ARCHITECTURE DRAWINGS

ARCHITEKTURZEICHNUNGEN
DISEÑOS DE ARQUITECTURA
DISEGNI D'ARCHITETTURA
PLANS D'ARCHITECTURE

ARCHITECTURE DRAWINGS

ARCHITEKTURZEICHNUNGEN
DISEÑOS DE ARQUITECTURA
DISEGNI D'ARCHITETTURA
PLANS D'ARCHITECTURE

THE PEPIN PRESS

Edited and produced by Dorine van den Beukel

ISBN 90 5496 041 8

The Pepin Press

POB 10349 • 1001 EH Amsterdam • The Netherlands

Tel (+) 31 20 4202021 • Fax (+) 31 20 4201152 • E-Mail pepin@euronet.nl

Printed in Singapore

Architecture Drawings

As with other volumes in The Pepin Press Design Series, this book is not meant to provide a complete architectural survey, but to offer (at a reasonable price) a vast collection of high-quality reproductions of important buildings such as churches, mosques, temples, houses, theatres, palaces, and public buildings, as a reference and source of inspiration for architects and designers.

All drawings in this publication date from the late nineteenth century. The presentation of this book follows the classical order of the history of architecture, as it was perceived by historians at that time; commencing with ancient Egyptian, Greek, and Roman architecture, followed by Early Christian, Byzantine, Moorish, Romanesque, Gothic, Renaissance, Baroque, and finally nineteenth-century architecture.

Many of the illustrations depict famous buildings, ranging from the Egyptian pyramids to the nineteenth-century Houses of Parliament in London, from the Acropolis in Athens to Europe's great Gothic cathedrals, and from the Hagia Sophia in Istanbul to Italian Renaissance palaces. However, there are also less renowned edifices shown here that are of considerable architectural interest: Roman tombs, medieval castles, seventeenth-century private houses, and public buildings dating from just before the turn of the twentieth century. In addition to the elevations, many buildings are shown complete with sections, plans and details.

It is particularly interesting that this book contains illustrations of several important structures that were still standing at the time these drawings were made, but have not survived to this day because they were neglected, abandoned, demolished or destroyed in war time. Many buildings that are now only known as ruins or archeological sites, such as ancient Greek temples or Roman theatres, are shown in their original state.

A complete list of all buildings can be found at the back of the book.

Architekturzeichnungen

Dieser fünfte Band der Serie Pepin Press Design Bücher gibt eine Vielzahl hochwertiger Reproduktionen wichtiger Gebäude wie Kirchen, Moscheen, Tempel, Häuser, Theater, Paläste und öffentliche Gebäude wieder, die Architekten und Designern als Referenzmaterial und Inspirationsquelle dienen.

Da alle Zeichnungen in diesem Buch aus dem späten 19. Jahrhundert stammen, ist der Inhalt nach den architekturgeschichtlichen Epochen geordnet, die von den Historikern jener Zeit benannt wurden; angefangen mit der Architektur der alten Ägypter, der Griechen und der Römer, gefolgt von der frühchristlichen, der byzantinischen und der maurischen Architektur, der Romanik, Gothik, Renaissance und Barock, bis hin zur Architektur des 19. Jahrhunderts.

Viele berühmte Gebäude der Architekturgeschichte werden aufgeführt – von den großen Pyramiden Ägyptens bis zu den Parlamentsgebäuden Londons des 19. Jahrhunderts, von der Akropolis in Athen bis zu den großen Kathedralen Europas, von der Hagia Sophia in Istanbul bis zu den großen Palästen der italienischen Renaissance. Aber auch weniger berühmte Bauten, die architektonisch jedoch von großem Interesse sind, werden hier dargestellt. Dazu zählen römische Grabstätten und mittelalterliche Burgen ebenso wie Bürgerhäuser aus dem 17. Jahrhundert und öffentliche Gebäude des späten 19. Jahrhunderts. Neben Gebäudegrundrissen enthält das Buch auch Schnitte, Oberansichten und Detailzeichnungen.

Besonderes Augenmerk verdienen Darstellungen wichtiger Gebäude, die zum Zeitpunkt ihrer Zeichnung noch standen, jedoch aufgrund von Verfall, Abriß oder Zerstörung im Krieg nicht erhalten geblieben sind. Von vielen Gebäuden, die heute nur als Ruinen oder archäologische Fundstätten bekannt sind, wie die Tempel der alten Griechen oder die Tempel der alten Römer, existieren Rekonstruktionen der Originalbauten.

Am Ende des Buches befindet sich ein vollständigen Verzeichnis sämtlicher Gebäude.

Plans d'architecture

A l'instar d'autres volumes de la série Design de Pepin Press, le but de cet ouvrage n'est pas de proposer une étude d'architecture complète mais d'offrir – à un prix raisonnable – une vaste collection de belles reproductions de grands édifices tels que des églises, des mosquées, des temples, des théâtres, des demeures, des palais et des édifices publics et de les présenter comme sources de référence et d'inspiration aux architectes et aux dessinateurs.

Toutes les reproductions datant de la fin du 19e siècle, cet ouvrage s'inscrit dans la ligne classique de l'histoire de l'architecture telle qu'elle fut perçue par les historiens de l'époque, c'est-à-dire depuis l'architecture de l'Antiquité égyptienne, grecque et romaine, suivie de celle du début du Christianisme, des époques byzantine, maure, romane, gothique, de la Renaissance et du Baroque, pour conclure avec l'architecture du 19e siècle.

Nombre de ces illustrations évoquent des monuments célèbres, des pyramides de l'ancienne Egypte aux Maisons du Parlement de Londres du 19e siècle, en passant par l'Acropole d'Athènes, les grandes cathédrales gothiques européennes, la basilique Sainte-Sophie d'Istanbul et les palais de la Renaissance italienne. Cet ouvrage témoigne également de réalisations moins connues mais présentant un fort intérêt architectural telles que des tombes romaines, des châteaux médiévaux, des bâtisses du 17e siècle ainsi que des édifices publics datant de la fin du 19e siècle. Outre les élévations, les représentations de nombreux édifices sont accompagnées de coupes, de plans, et de détails.

Cet ouvrage se singularise également par la présentation de diverses structures importantes qui étaient encore en état à l'époque où elles furent dessinées, mais qui ont depuis disparu par fait de négligence, d'abandon ou qui furent démolies ou détruites par les guerres. Ce livre inclut aussi des reconstitutions rappelant l'apparence initiale de nombreux édifices qui aujourd'hui sont ruines ou sites archéologiques, tels que les théâtres et les temples de la Rome ou de la Grèce antique.

Une liste exhaustive de tous les édifices figure au dos du livre.

Disegni d'architettura

Come per gli altri volumi in The Pepin Press Design Series, l'intento di questo libro non è di fornire una rassegna completa di architettura, ma di offrire – a un prezzo ragionevole – un'ampia collezione di riproduzioni di alta qualità di edifici importanti come chiese, moschee, templi, case, teatri, palazzi ed edifici pubblici, che sono serviti da fonti di riferimento e ispirazione per architetti e designer.

Dato che tutti i disegni in questa pubblicazione risalgono alla fine dell'Ottocento, l'orizzonte di questo libro viene definito dall'ordine classico della storia dell'architettura, così come veniva concepita dagli storici del tempo; all'inizio c'era l'architettura egiziana, greca e romana, seguita da quella paleo-cristiana, bizantina, araba, romanica, gotica, rinascimentale, barocca e infine dall'architettura dell'Ottocento.

Molte delle illustrazioni presentano edifici famosi, dalle piramidi d'Egitto fino all'ottocentesco Parlamento di Londra, dall'Acropoli di Atene alle grandi cattedrali gotiche europee, e da S. Sofia a Istanbul ai palazzi del Rinascimento italiano. Tuttavia, qui vengono rappresentati anche edifici meno noti, che sono di grande interesse architettonico, come tombe romane, castelli medievali, case private del Seicento, ed edifici pubblici che datano dalla fine del secolo scorso. Oltre ai prospetti, molti edifici vengono mostrati completi in sezioni, piante e dettagli.

Di particolare interesse è il fatto che questo libro contiene delle rappresentazioni di numerosi importanti strutture che esistevano ancora quando questi disegni vennero eseguiti, ma non sono sopravvissuti fino a oggi perché vennero trascurati, abbandonati, demoliti o distrutti in tempo di guerra. Di molti edifici che oggi sono noti solo come rovine o siti archeologici, come i templi dell'antica Grecia o i teatri romani, vengono presentate le riproduzioni del loro stato originale.

Alla fine del libro si può trovare un elenco completo di tutti gli edifici.

Diseños de Arquitectura

El quinto volúmen de la Serie de Diseño de Pepin Press, ofrece una inmensa colección de reproducciones de alta calidad de importantes edificios como iglesias, mezquitas, templos, casas, teatros, palacios y edificios públicos, y ser con ello una obra de referencia y fuente de inspiración para arquitectos y diseñadores.

Como todos los dibujos de esta publicación datan de finales del siglo diecinueve, el alcance de este libro es definido por el orden clásico de la historia de la arquitectura tal como la percibían los historiadores de entonces, comenzando con la antigua arquitectura egipcia, griega y romana, seguida de la primitiva cristiana, bizantina, mora, románica, gótica, renacentista, barroca, y finalmente la arquitectura del siglo diecinueve.

Muchas de las ilustraciones exhiben famosos edificios, desde las pirámides egipcias hasta las Cámaras del Parlamento del siglo diecinueve en Londres, desde la Acrópolis en Atenas hasta las grandes catedrales góticas de Europa, y desde la catedral de Santa Sofía en Estambul hasta los palacios del Renacimiento italiano. Sin embargo, también se representan edificios de menos renombre, pero que son de gran interés arquitectónico, como sepulcros romanos, castillos medievales, casas privadas del siglo diecisiete, y edificios públicos datando de justo antes del comienzo del siglo veinte. Además de los alzados, muchos edificios aparecen completos con secciones, planos y detalles.

De particular interés es que este libro contiene representaciones de varias estructuras importantes que estaban aún de pie cuando se hicieron estos dibujos, pero que no han sobrevivido hasta el día de hoy debido a descuido, abandono, demolición o a destrucción en tiempo de guerra. En el caso de muchos edificios que hoy sólo son conocidos como ruinas o emplazamientos arqueológicos, como antiguos templos griegos o teatros romanos, se muestran reconstrucciones en su estado original.

Al final del libro se encuentra una lista completa de todos los edificios.

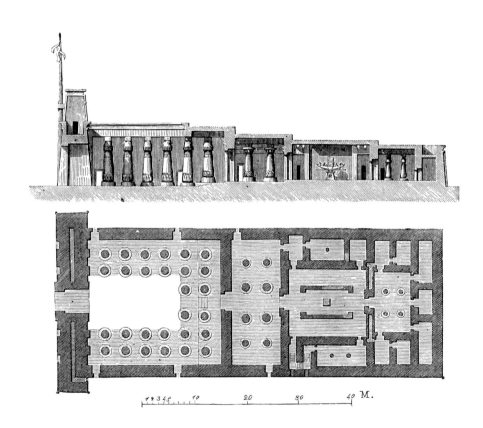

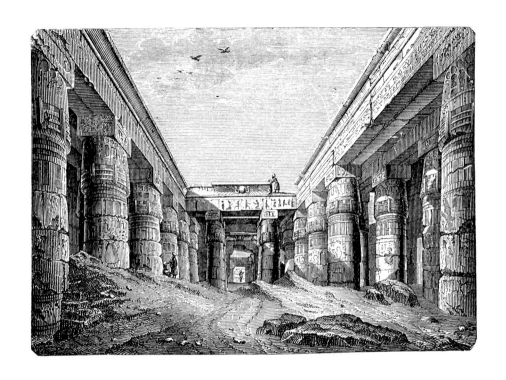

14

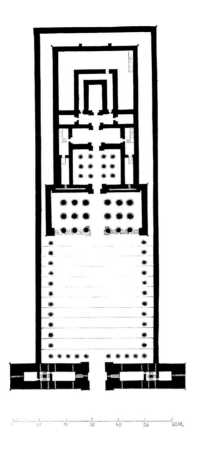

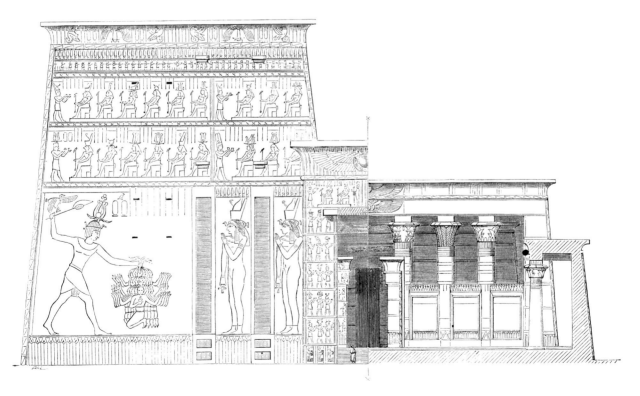

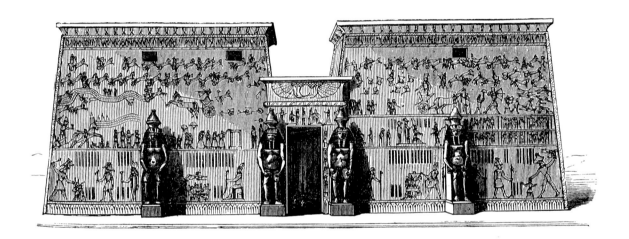

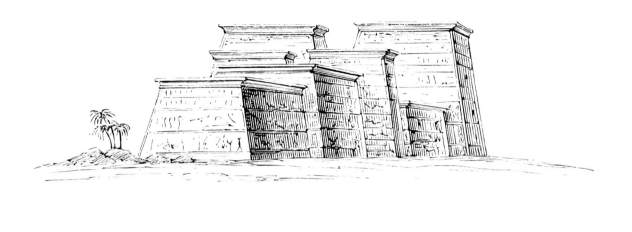

18

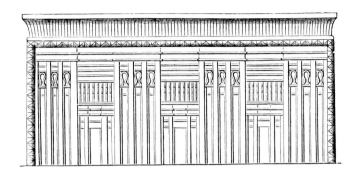

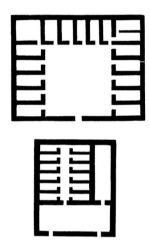

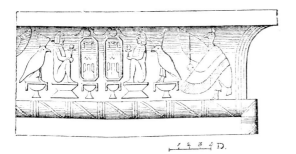

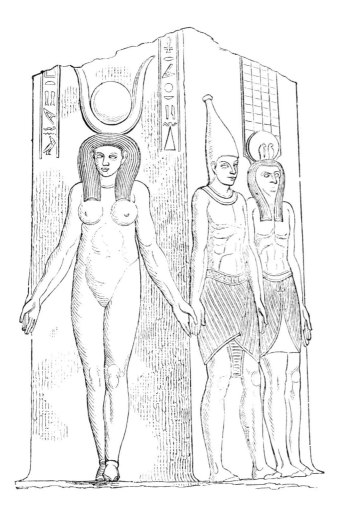

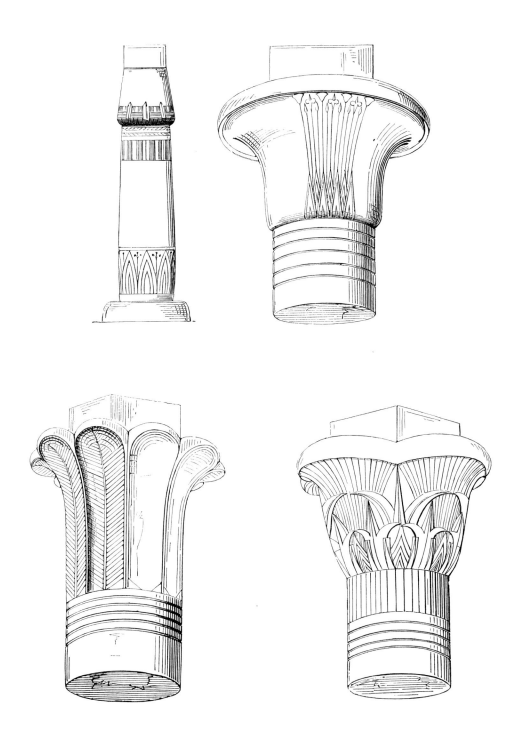

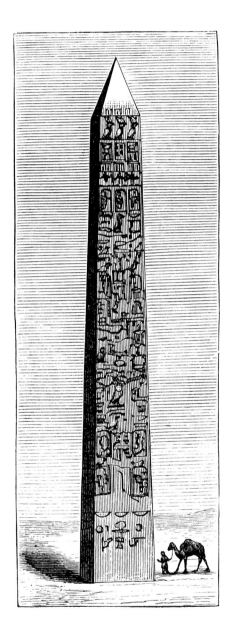

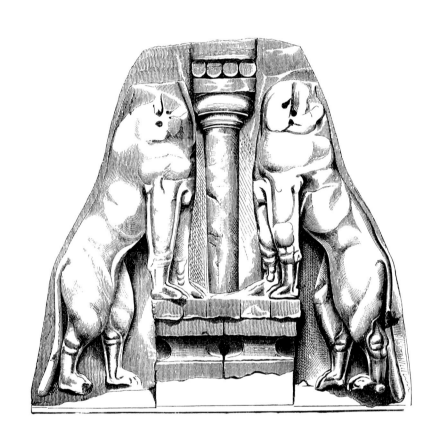

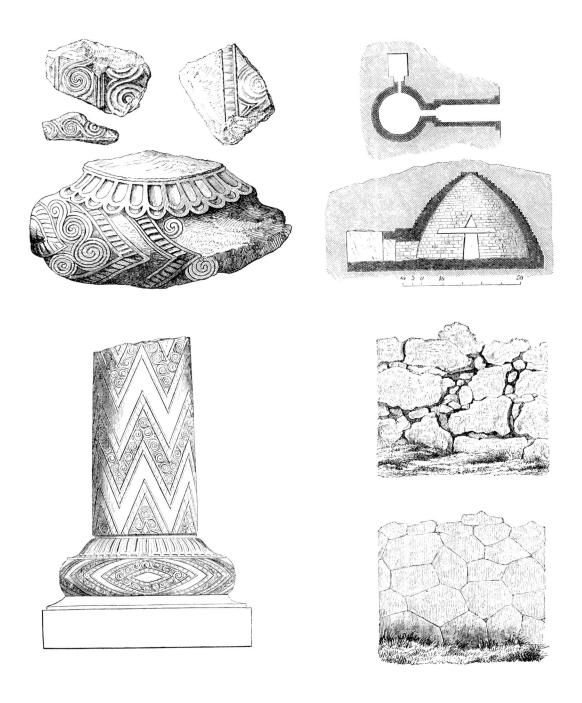

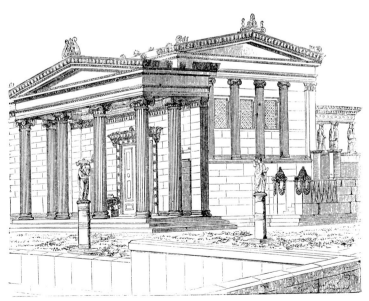

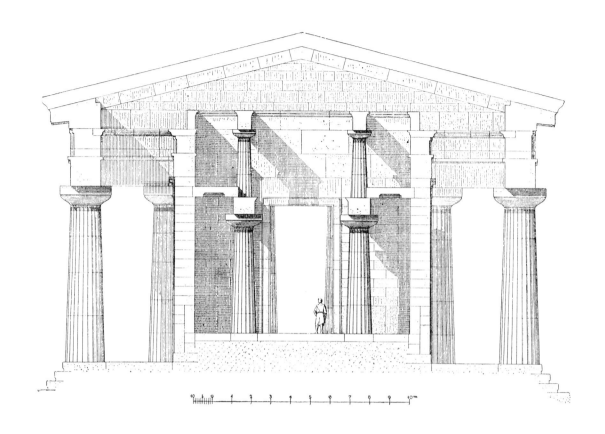

36

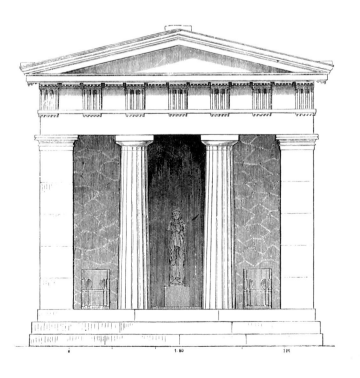

37

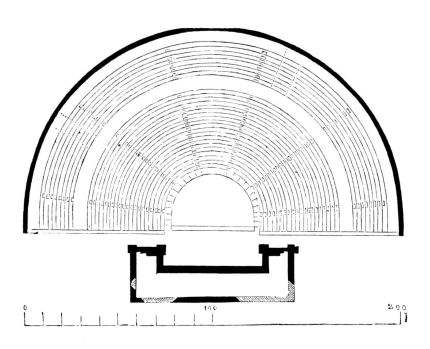

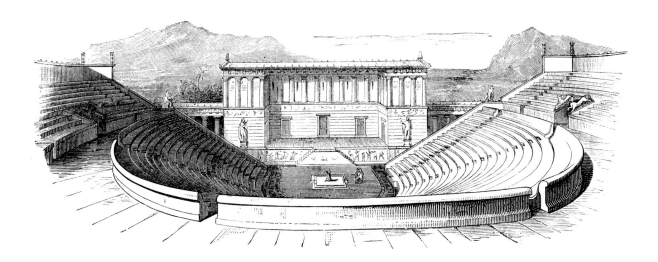

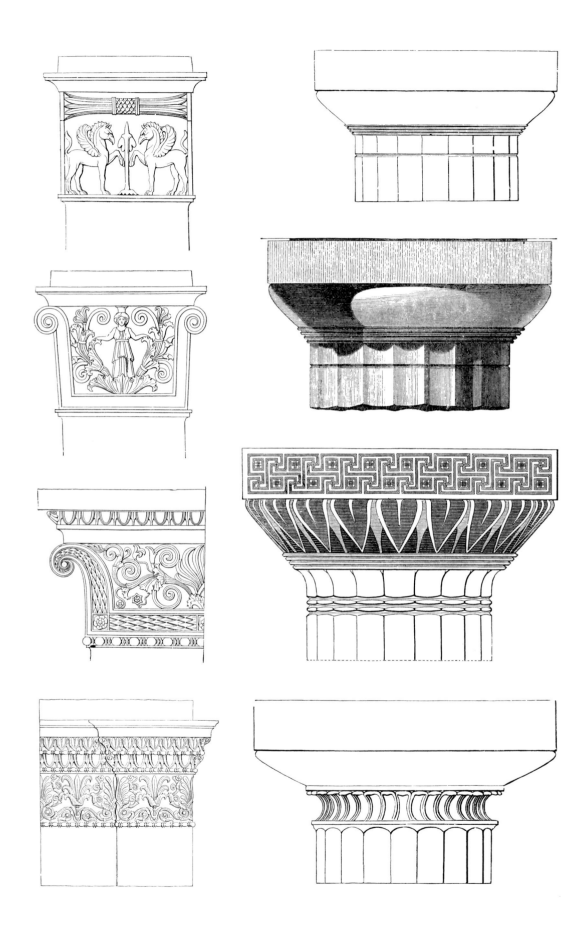

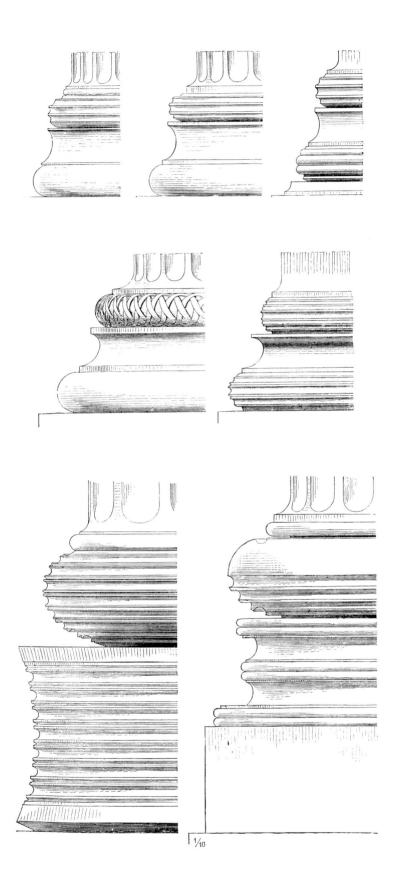

1/10

43

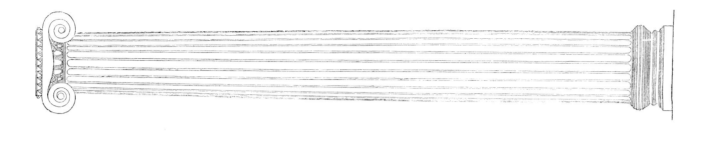

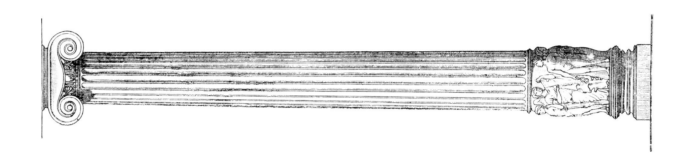

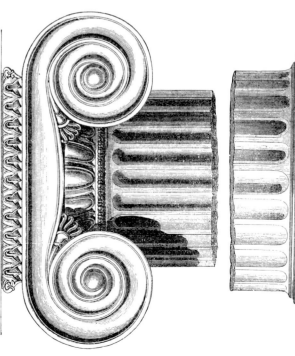

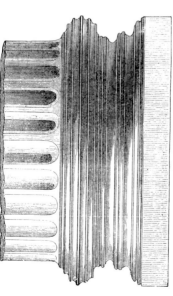

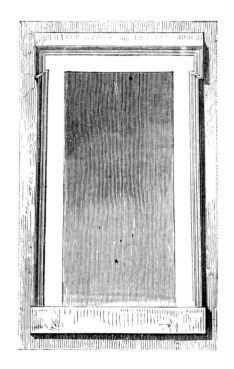

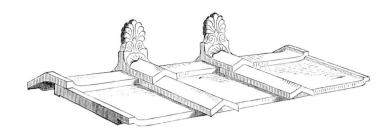

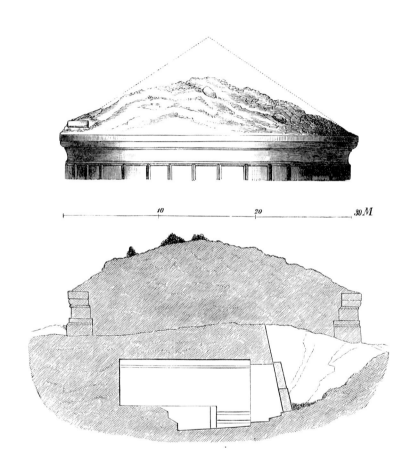

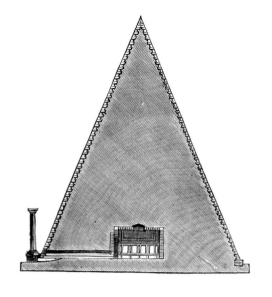

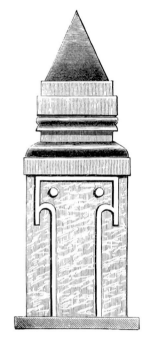

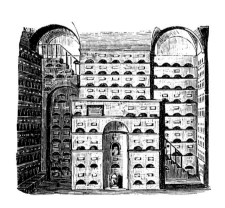

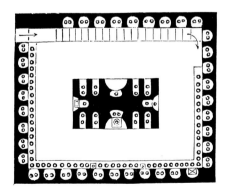

$30\ M$.

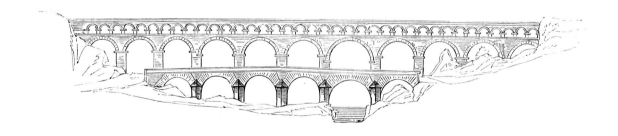

61

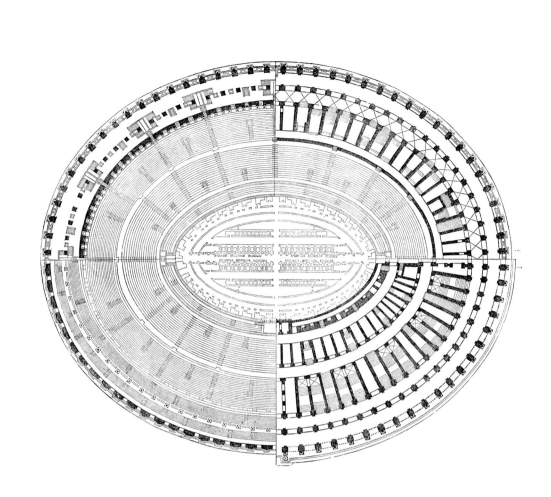

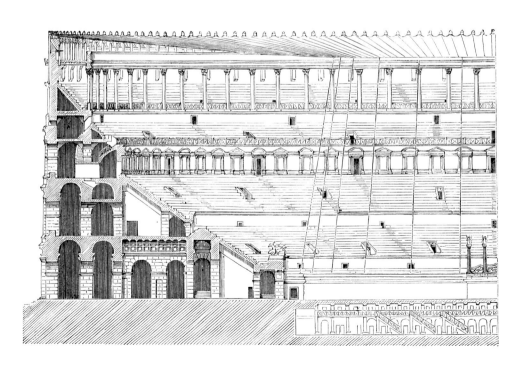

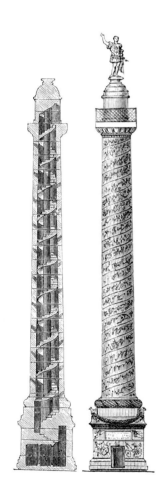

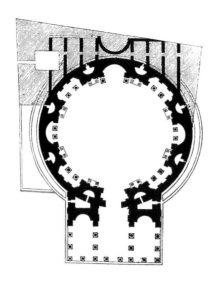

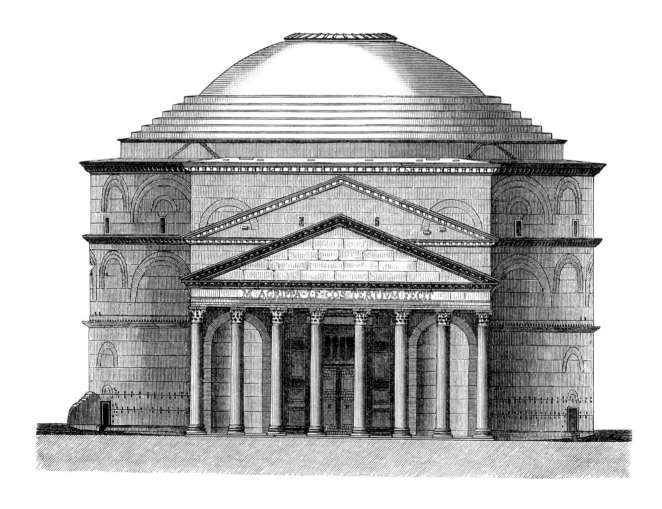

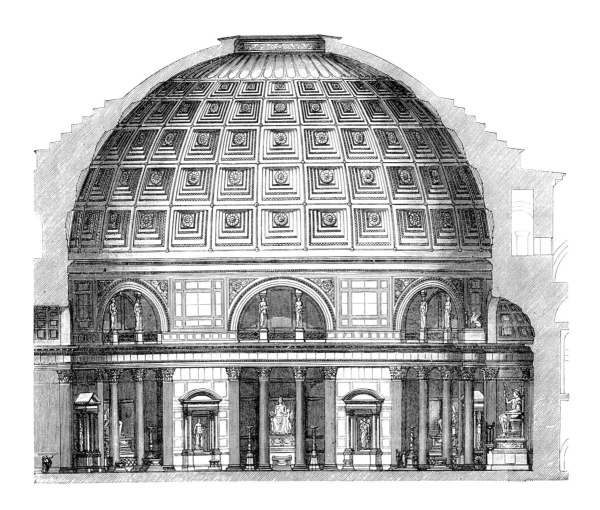

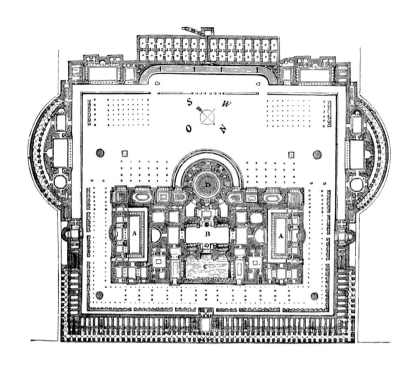

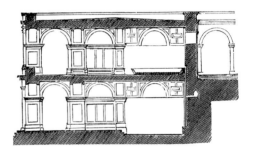

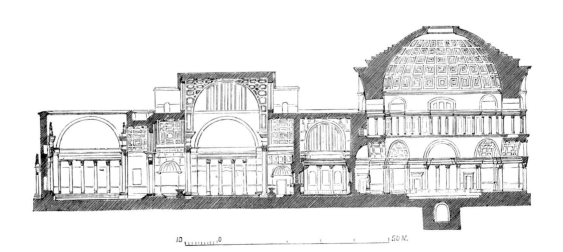

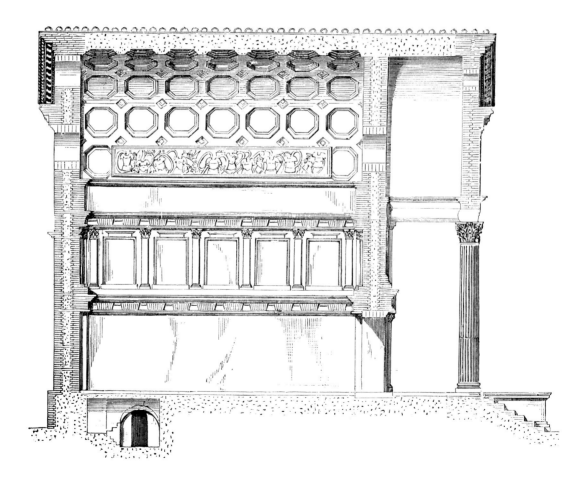

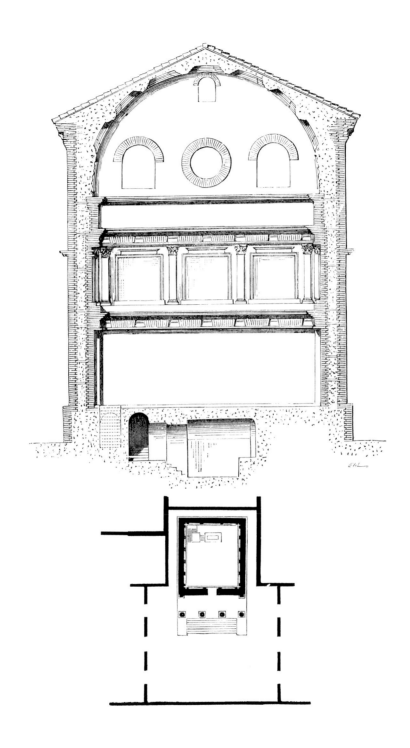

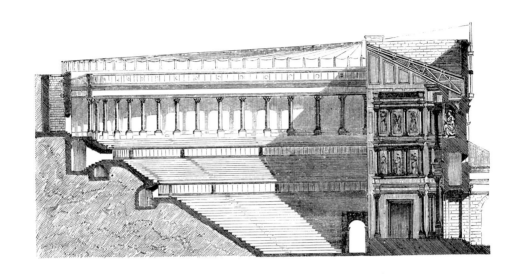

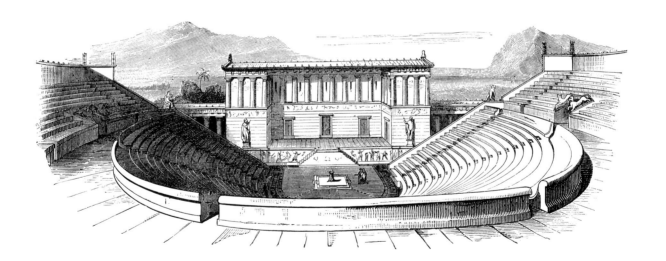

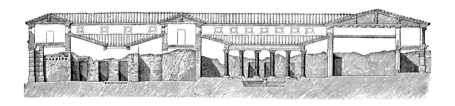

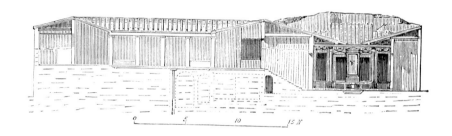

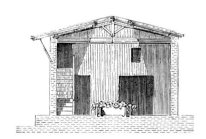

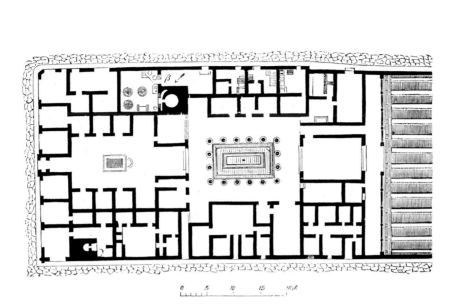

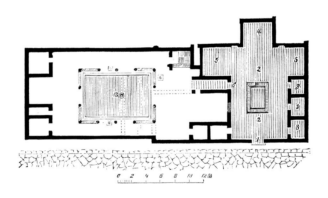

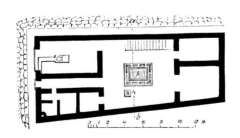

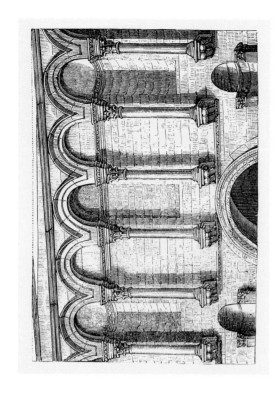

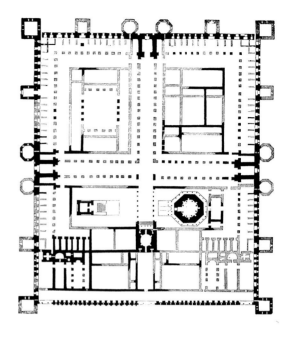

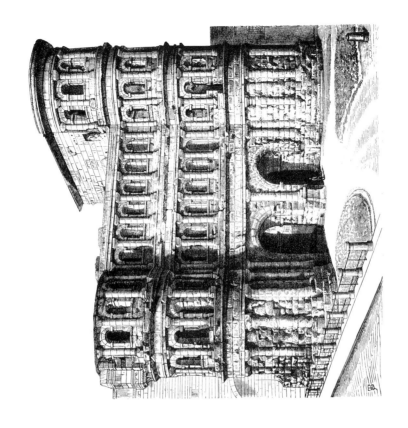

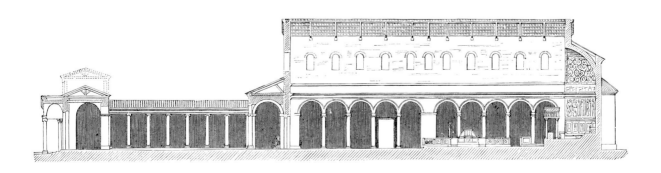

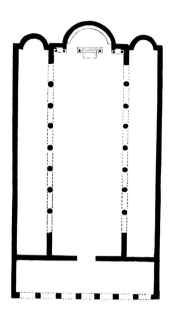

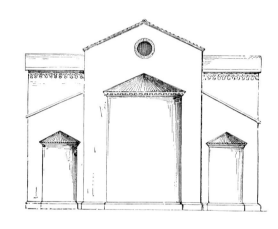

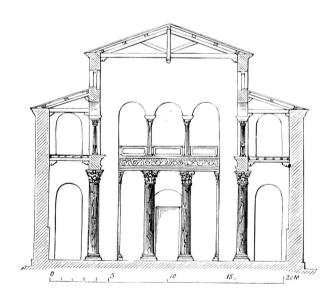

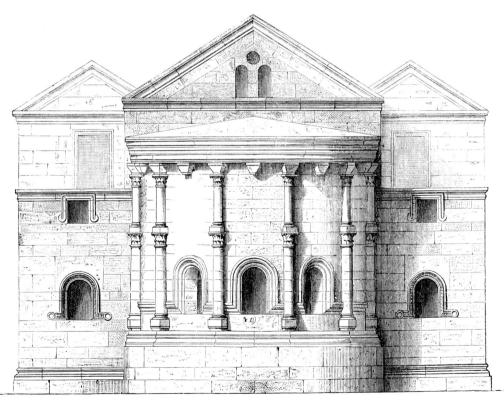

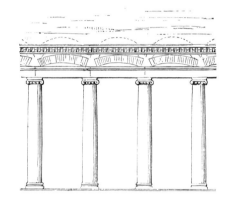

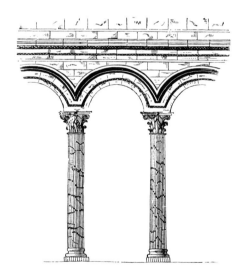

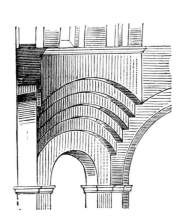

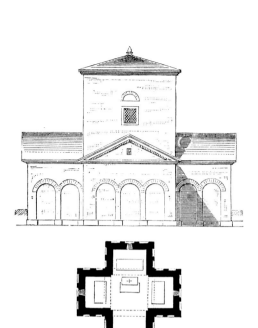

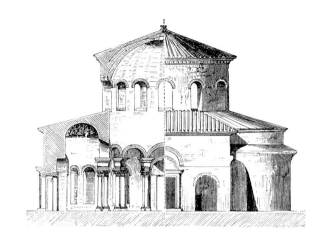

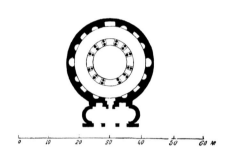

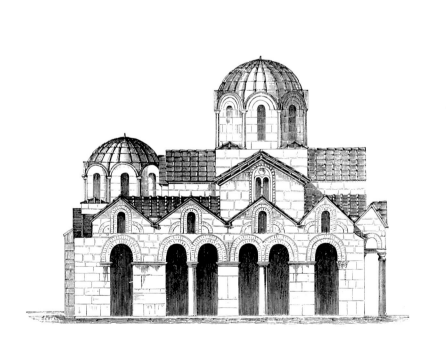

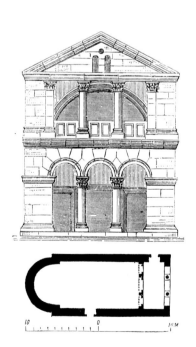

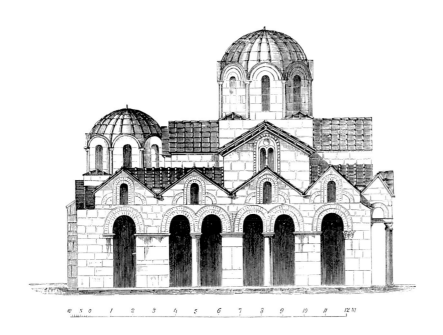

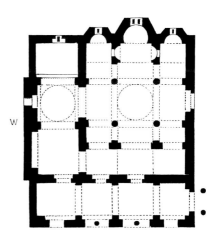

W

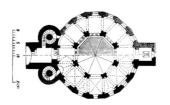

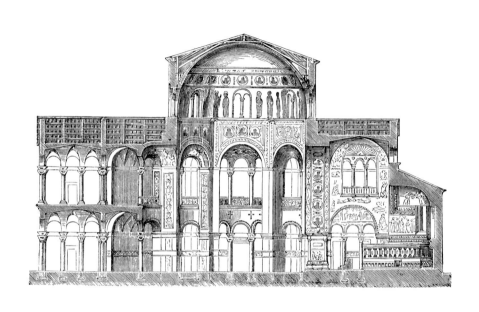

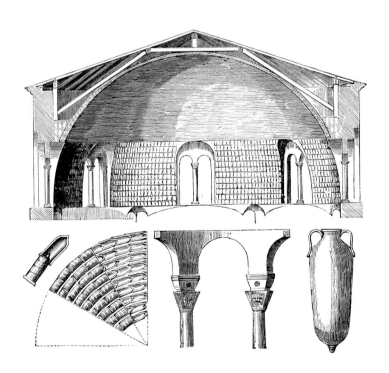

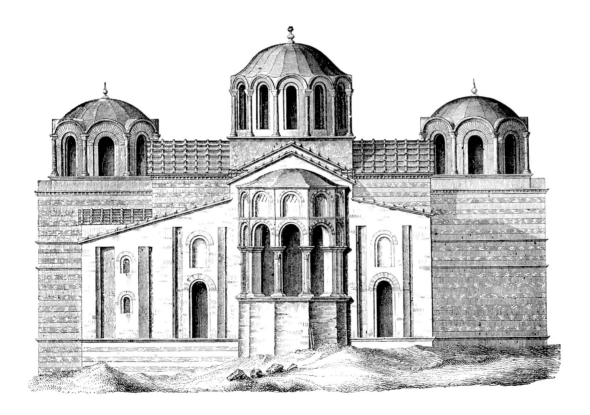

98

0   5   10   20   30   40   50   60 M

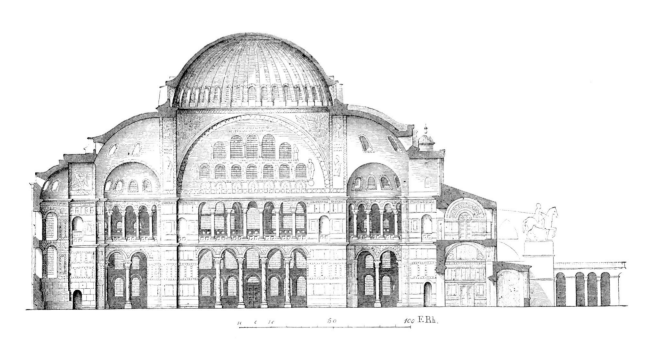

0   5   10   50   100 F.Rh.

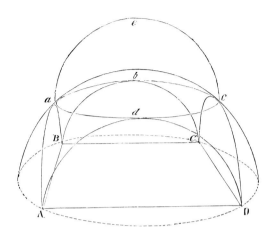

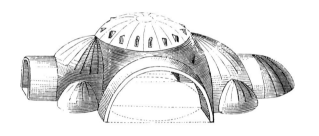

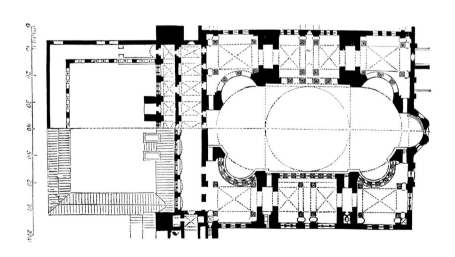

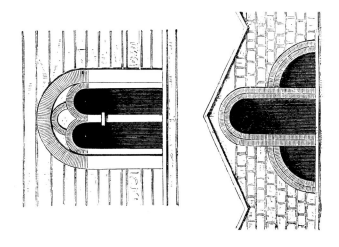

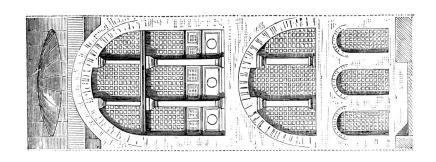

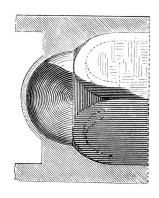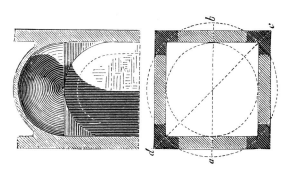

103

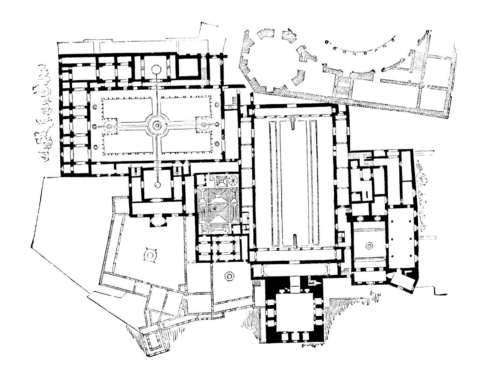

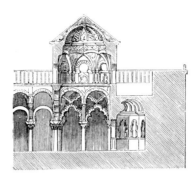

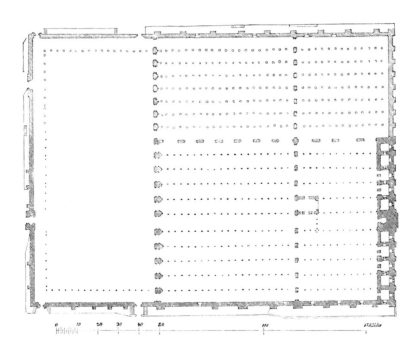

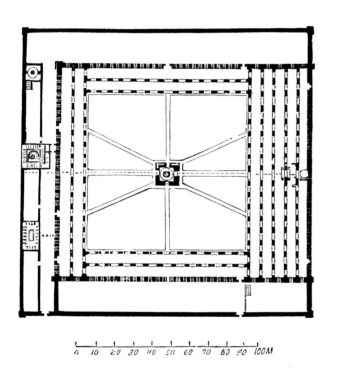

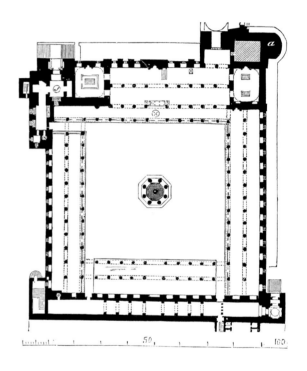

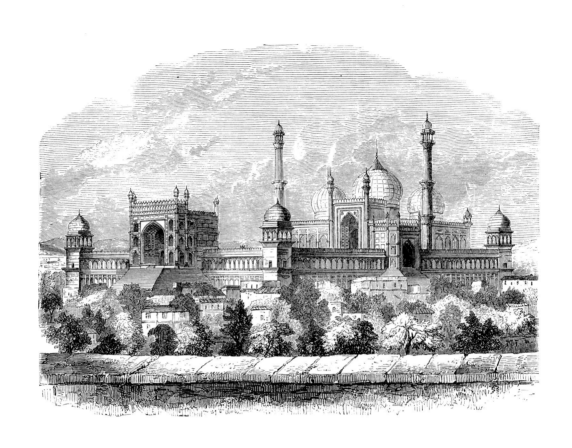

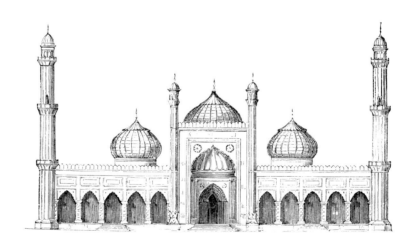

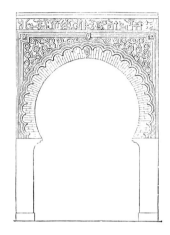

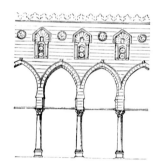

117

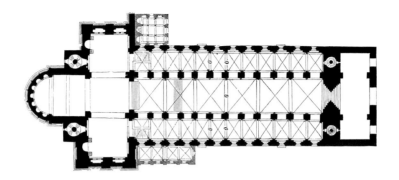

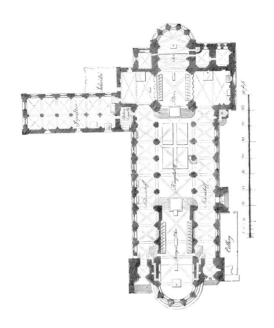

121

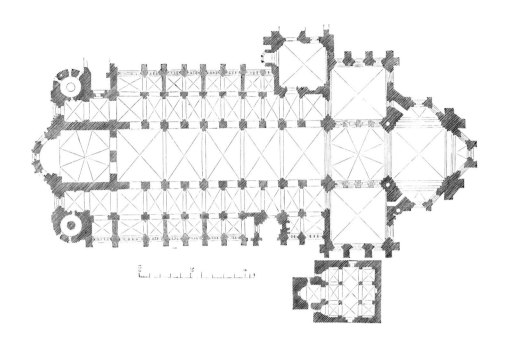

124

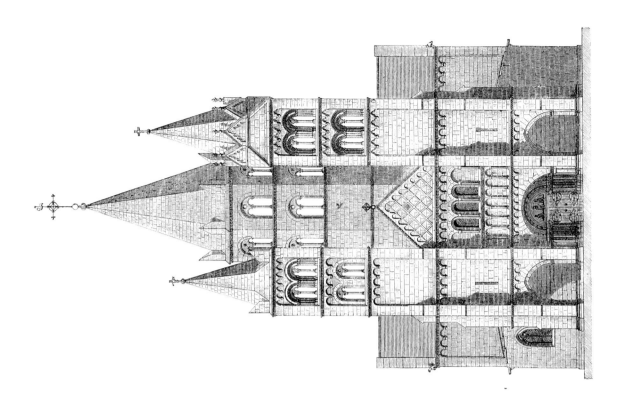

126

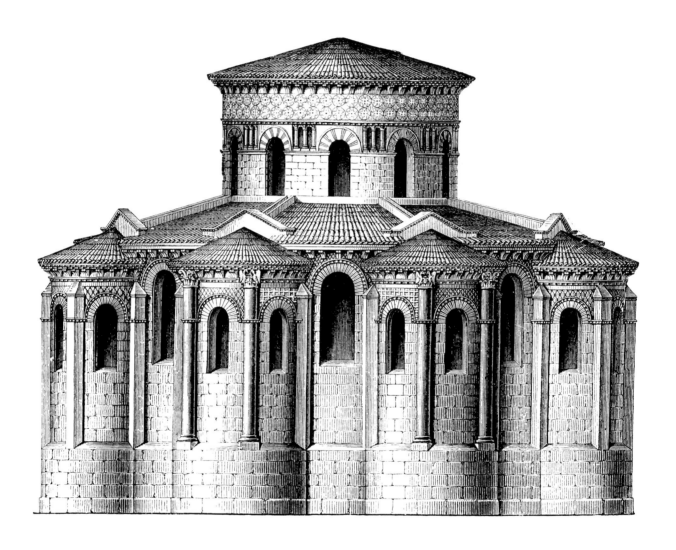

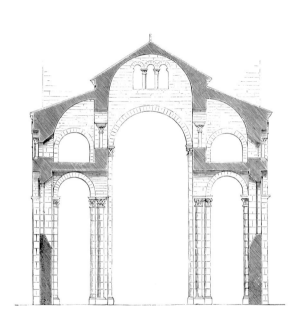

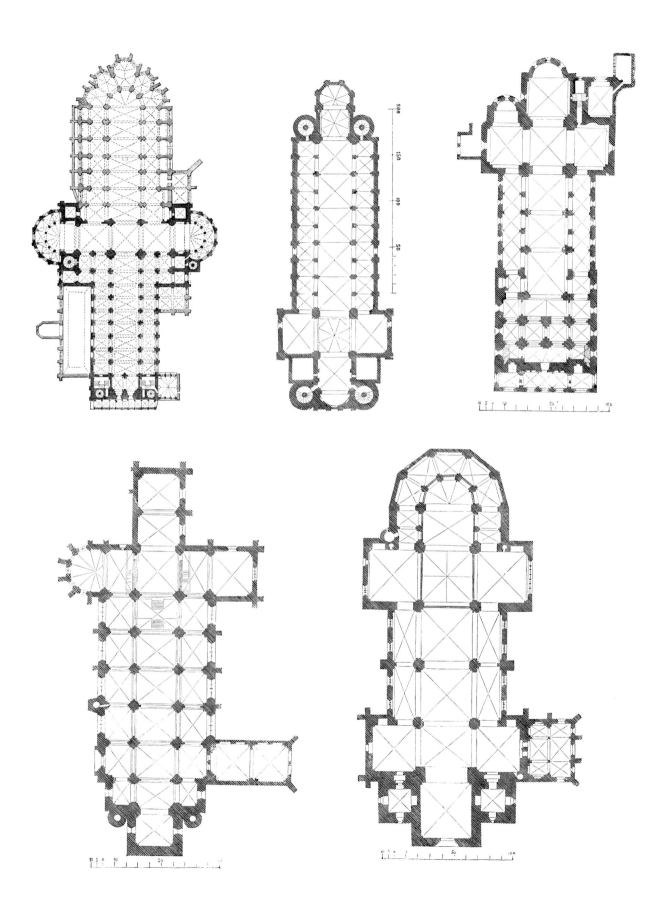

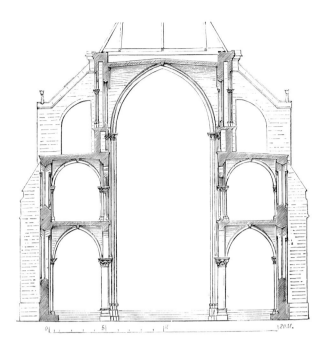

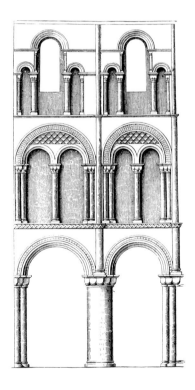

131

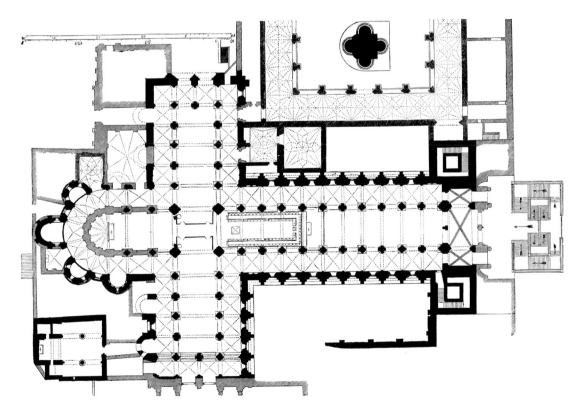

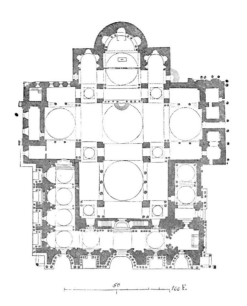

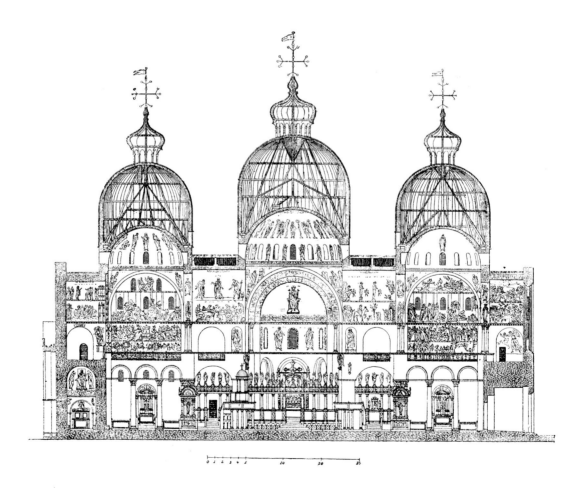

139

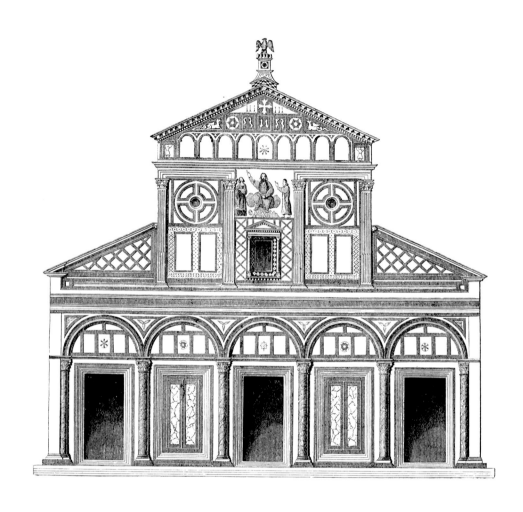

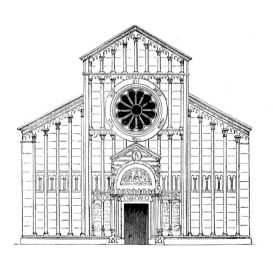

142

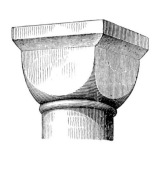

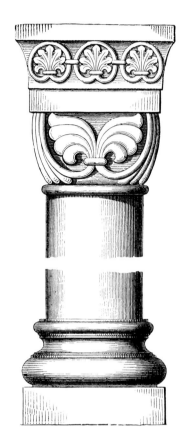

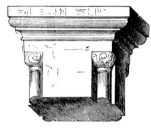

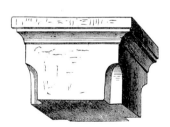

144

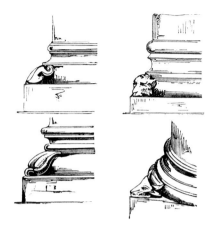

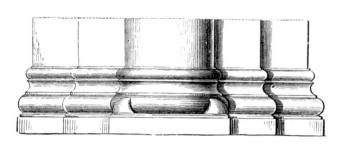

147

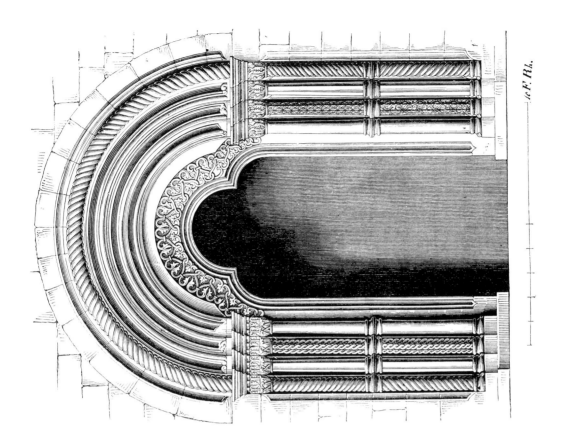

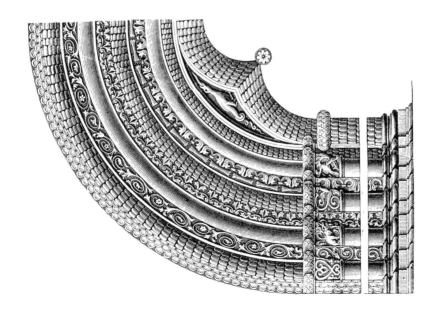

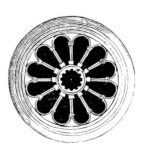

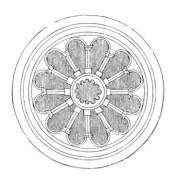

153

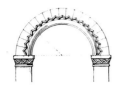

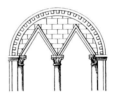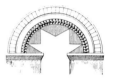

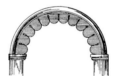

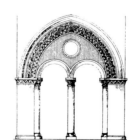

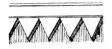   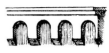

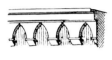  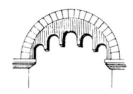 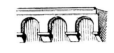

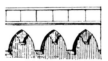

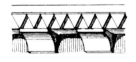  

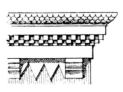 

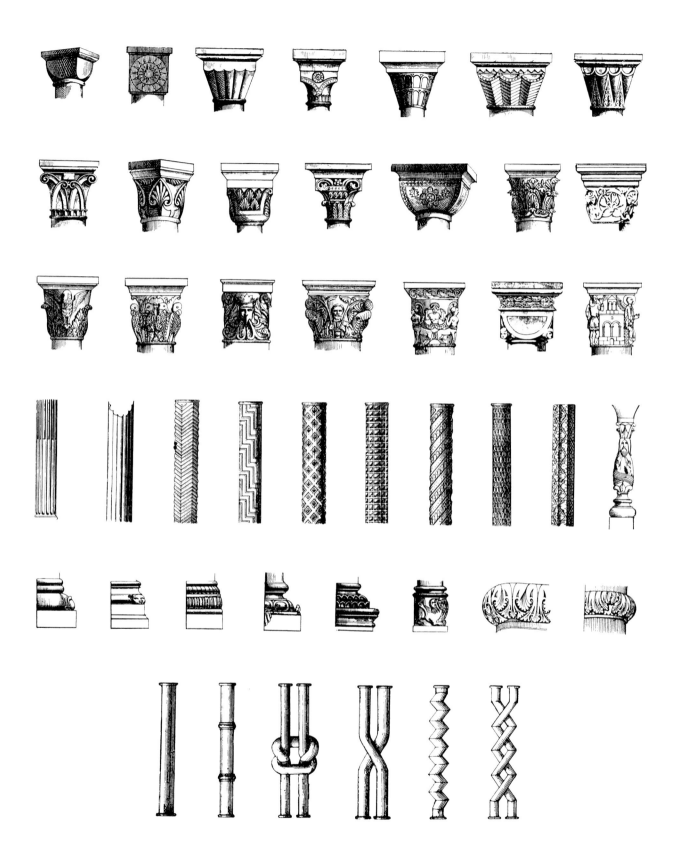

156

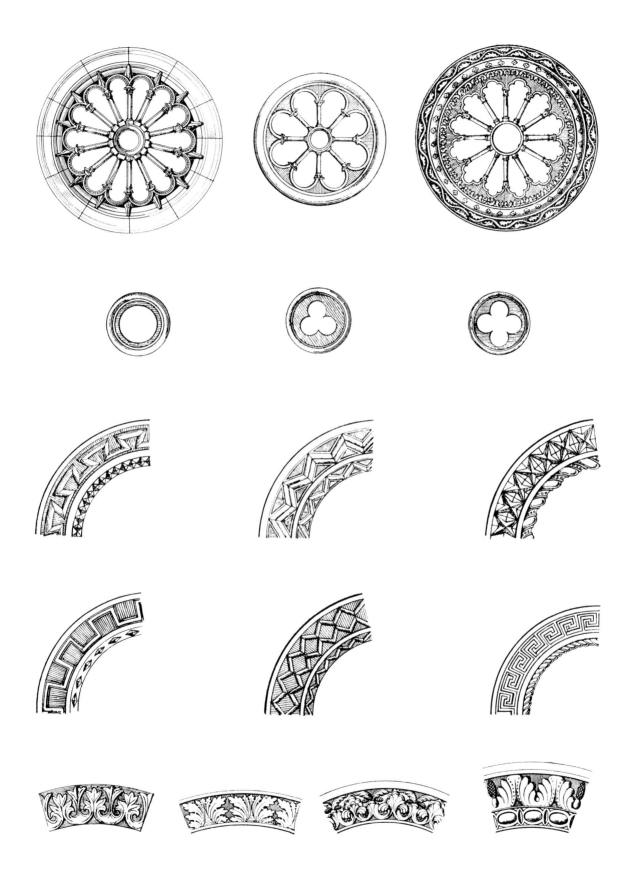

162

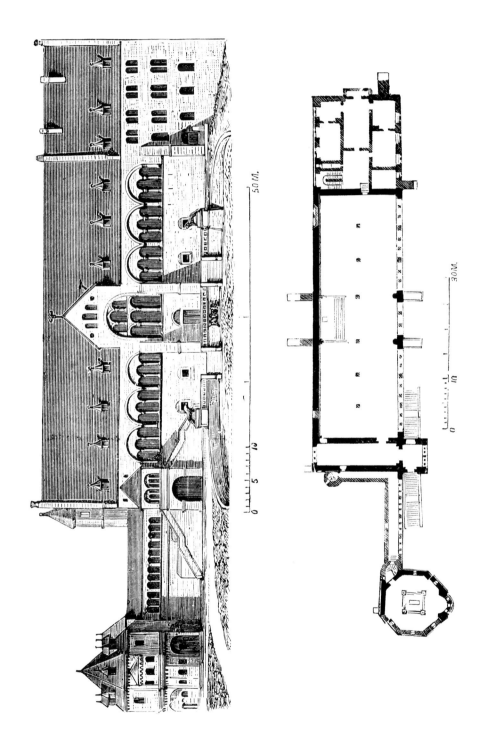

165

5 m

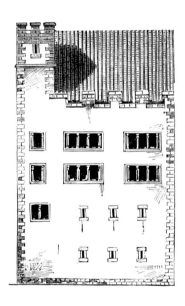

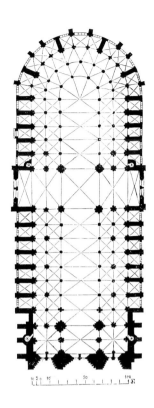

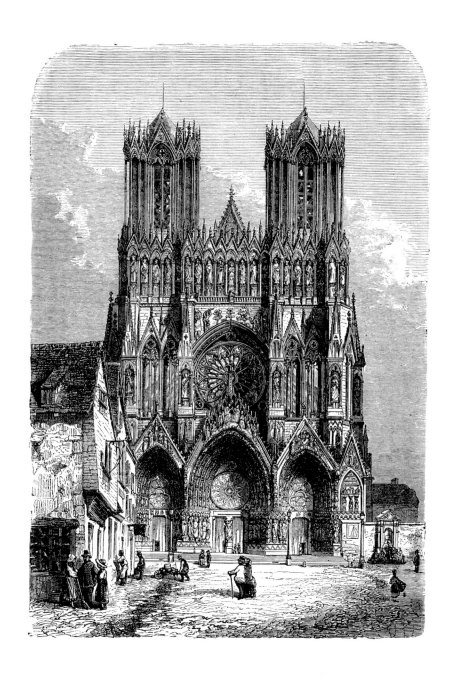

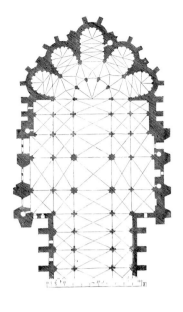

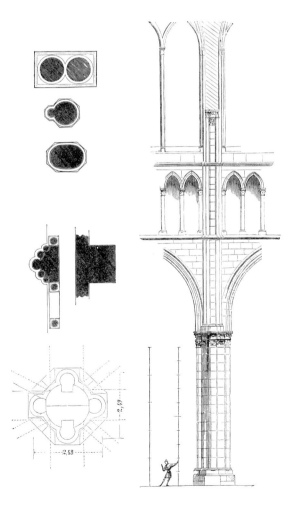

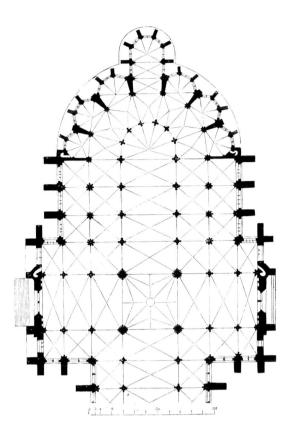

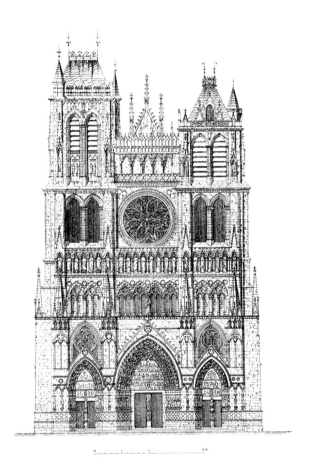

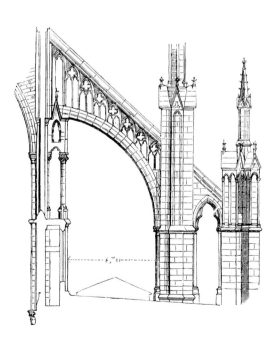

173

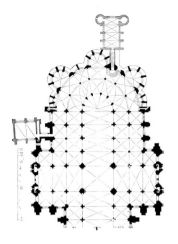

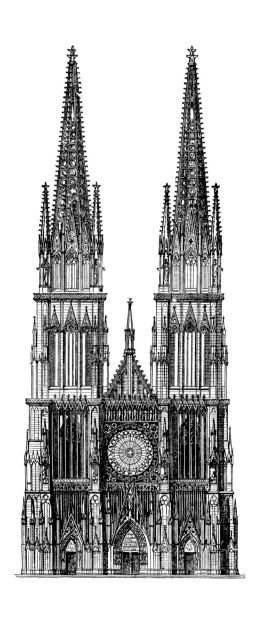

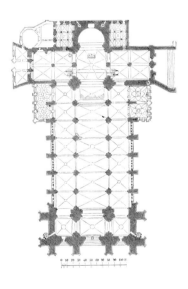

30 M.

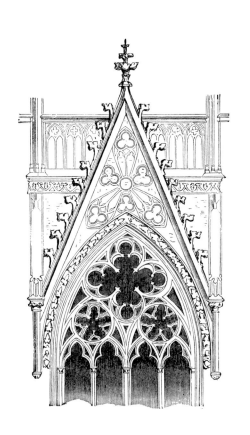

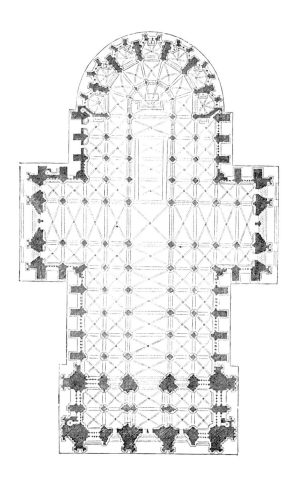

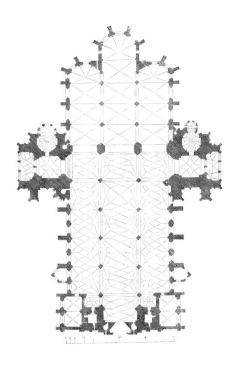

184

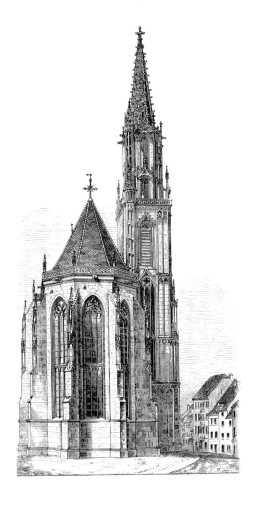

185

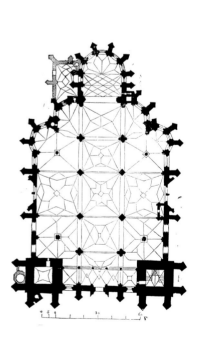

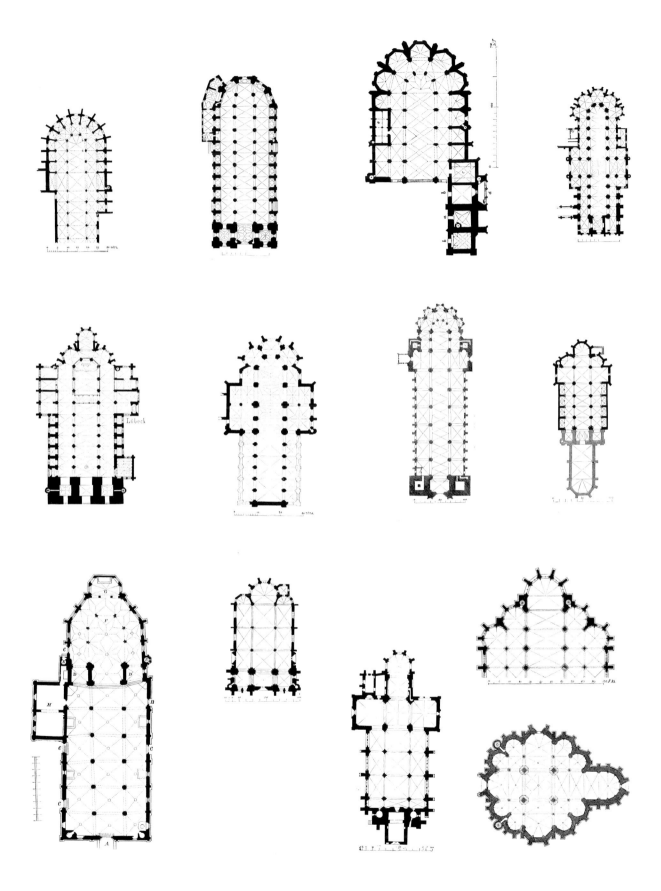

187

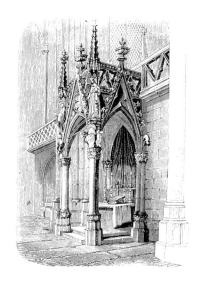 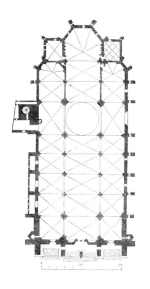 

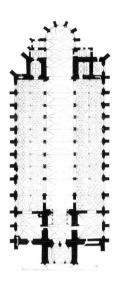

189

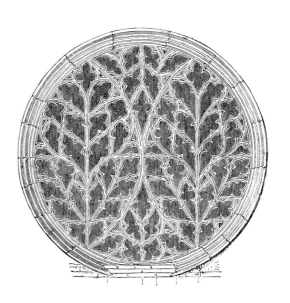

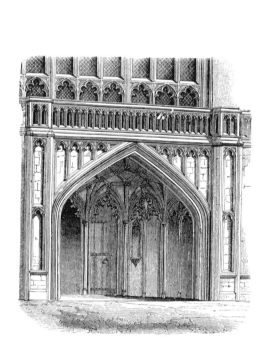

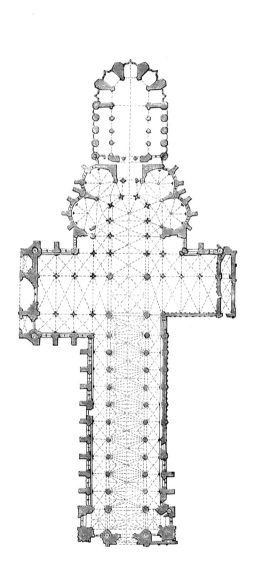

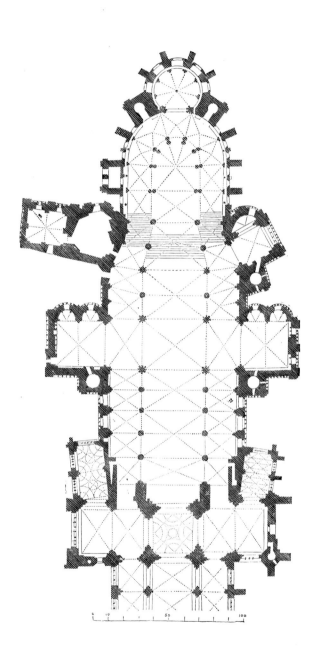

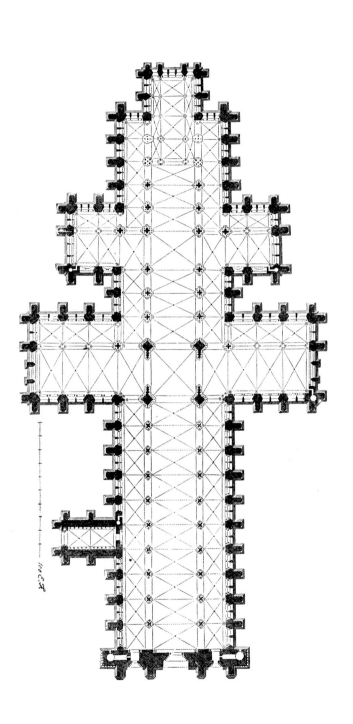

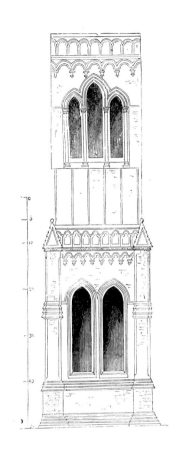

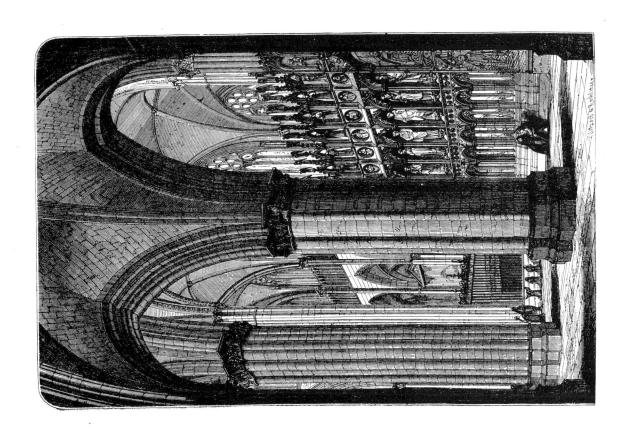

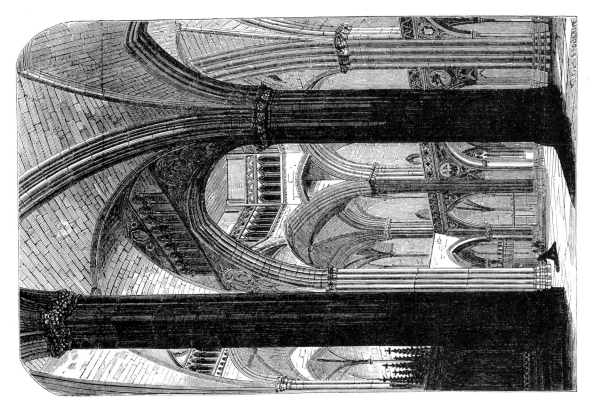

199

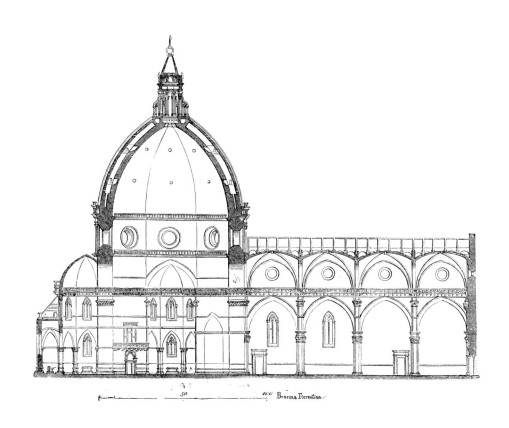

50   100   Bracena Florentina.

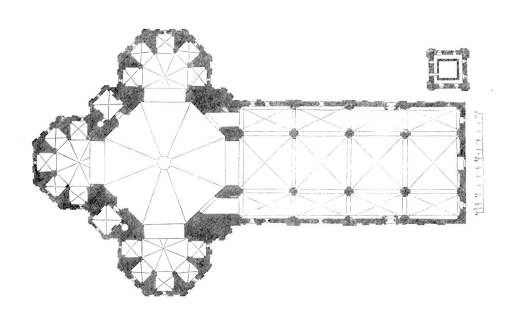

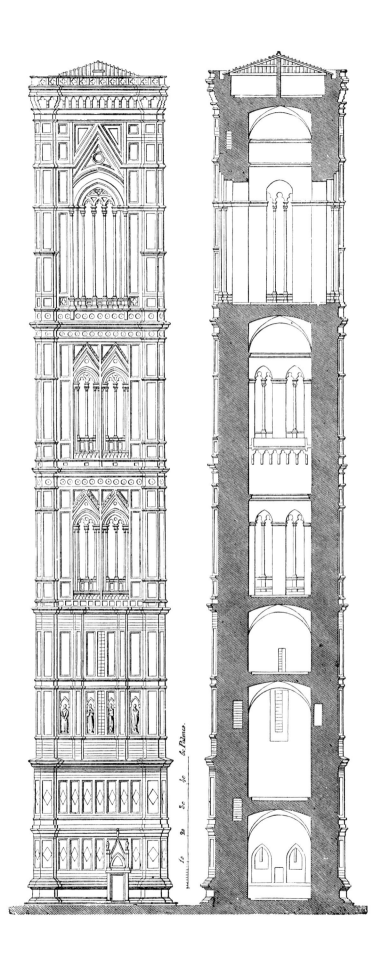

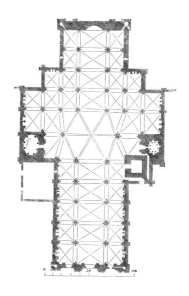

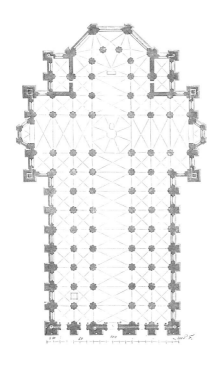

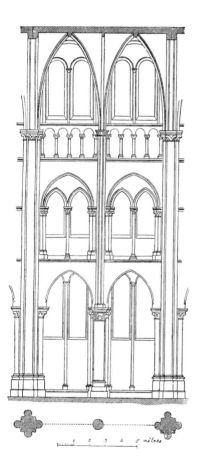

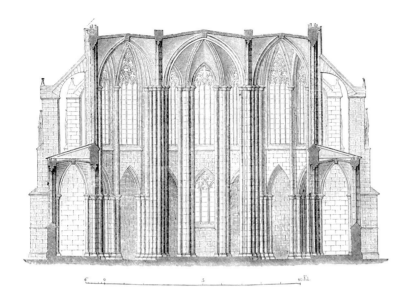

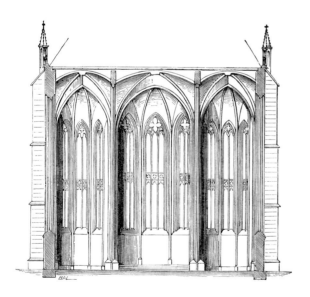

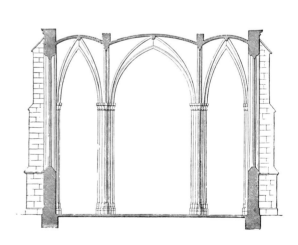

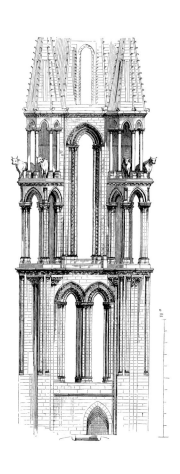

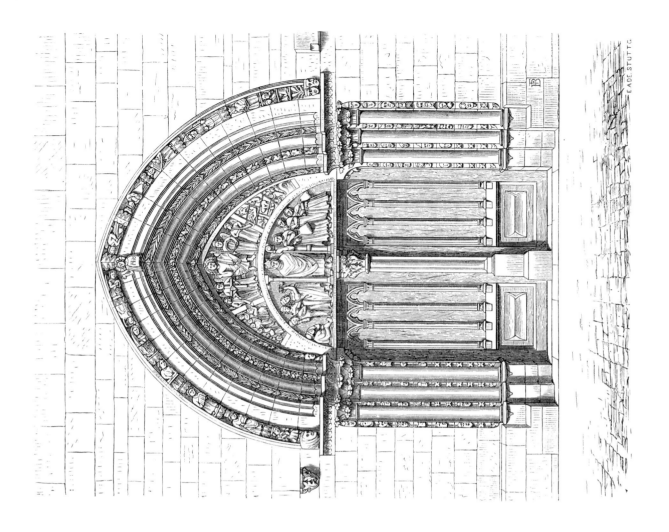

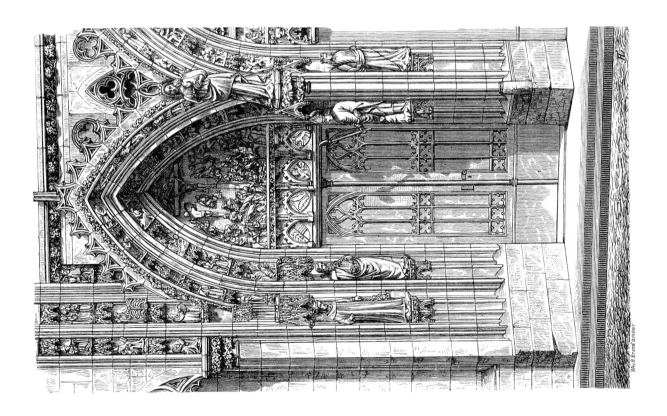

213

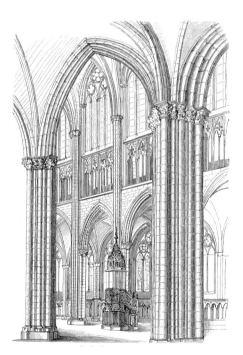

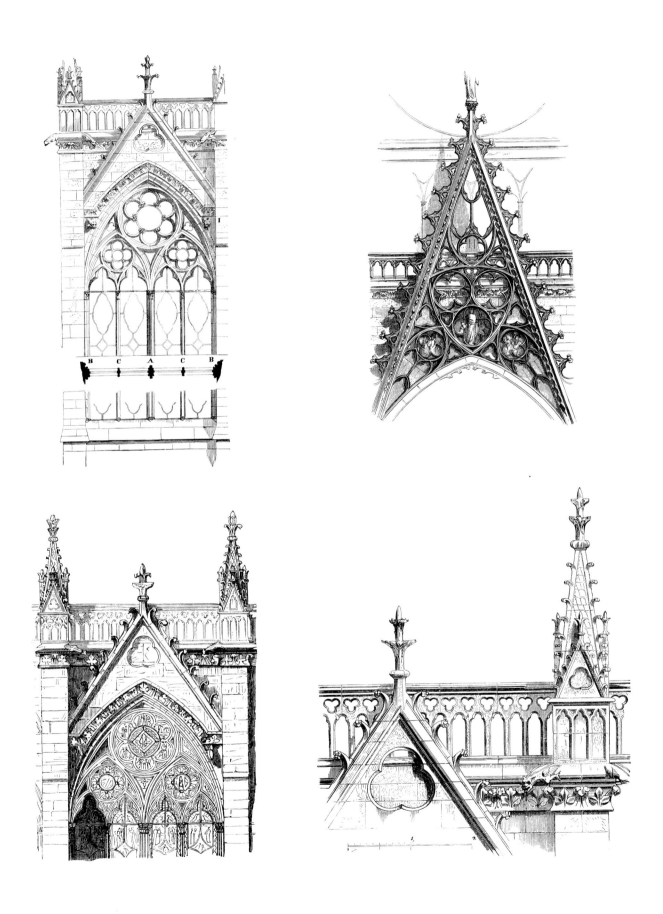

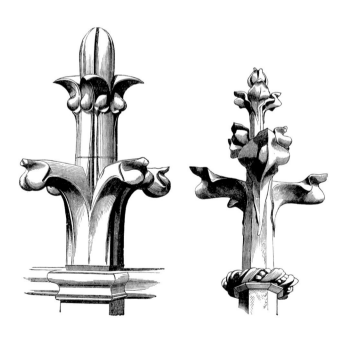

221

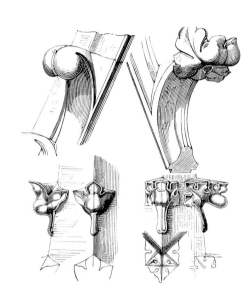

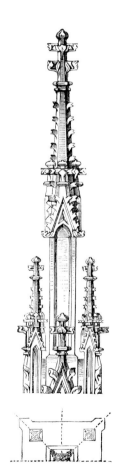

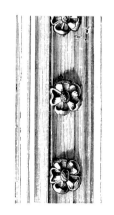

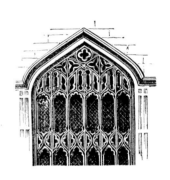

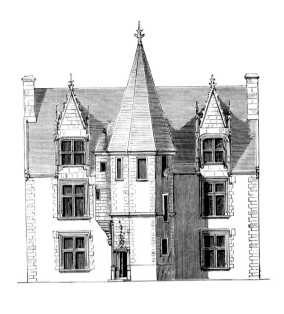

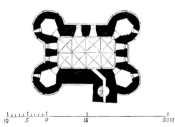

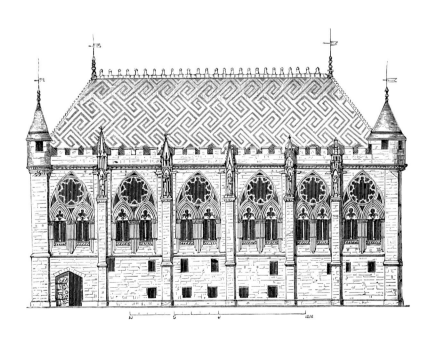

225

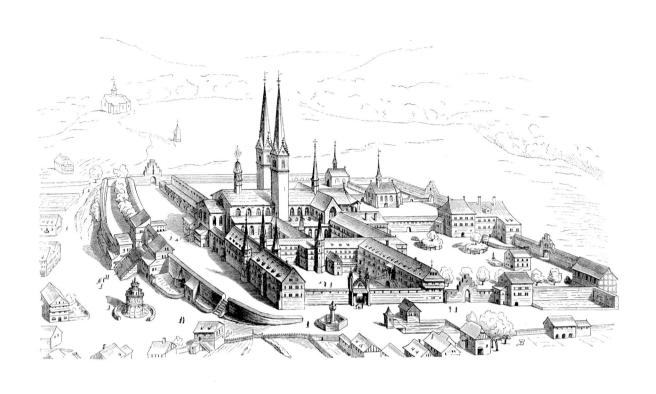

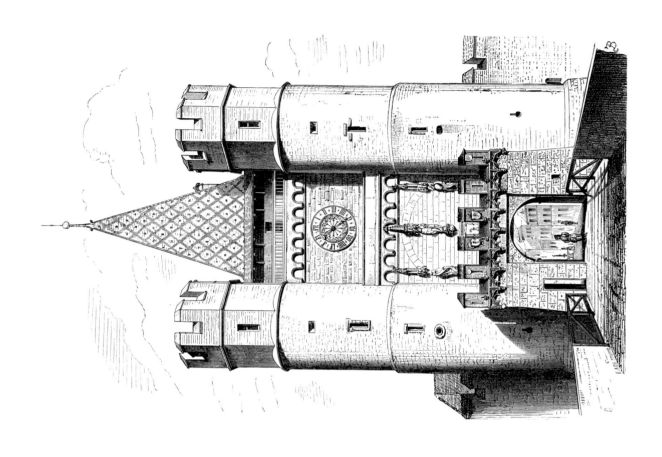

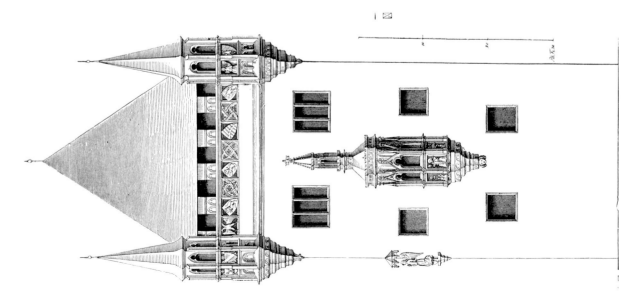

228

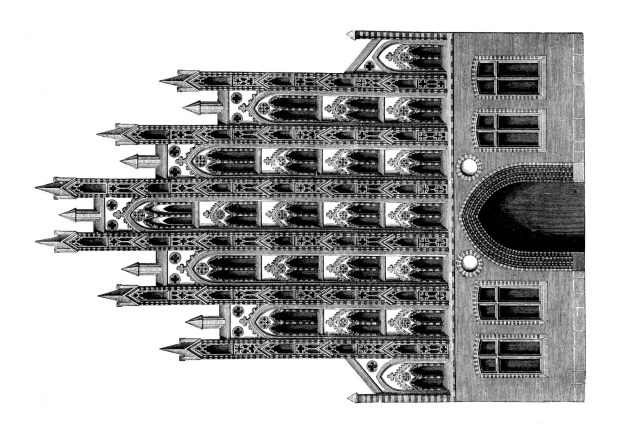

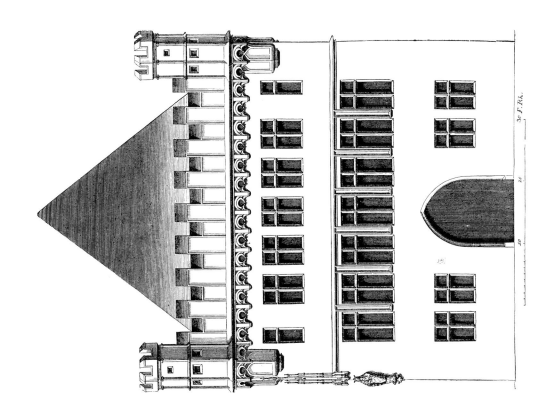

Münster

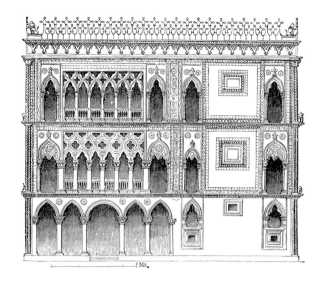

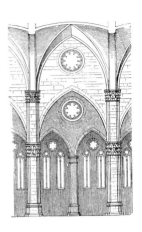
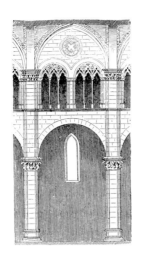
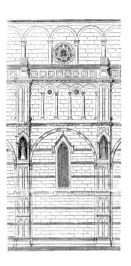

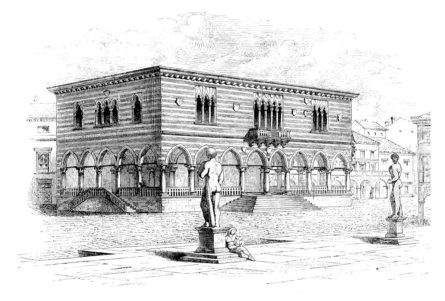

235

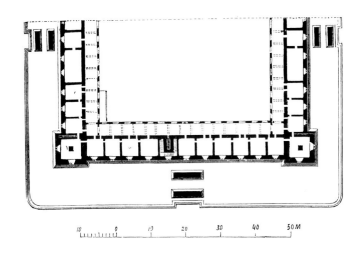

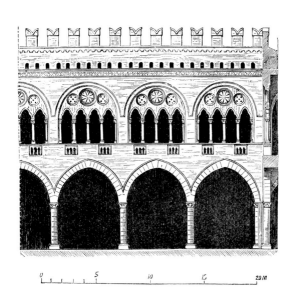

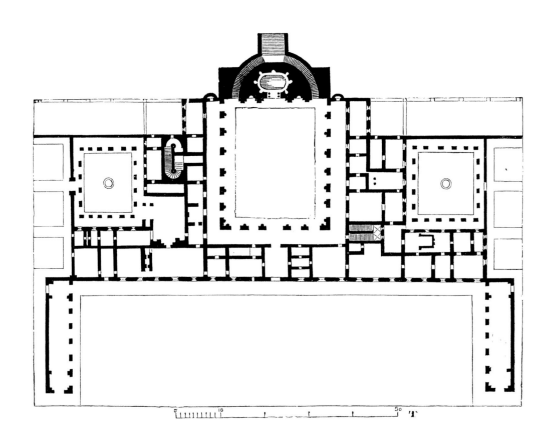

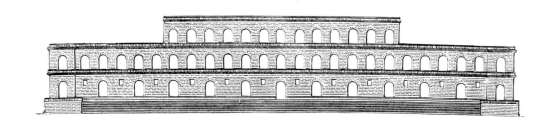

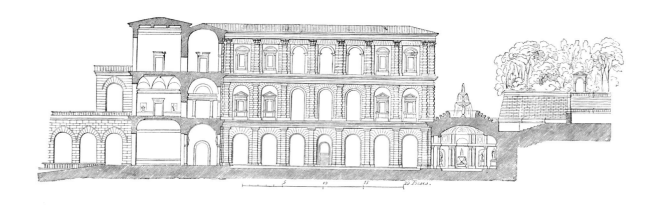

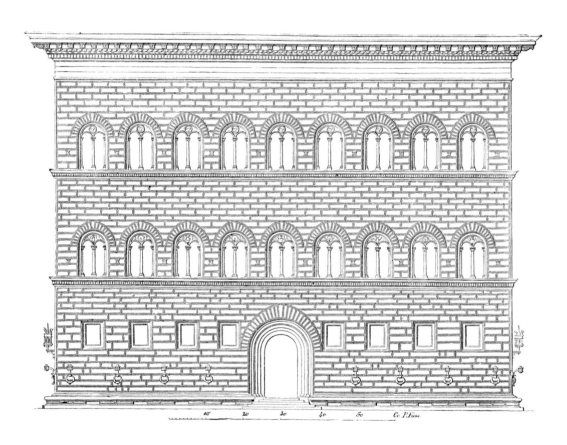

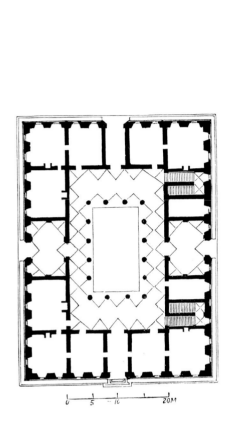

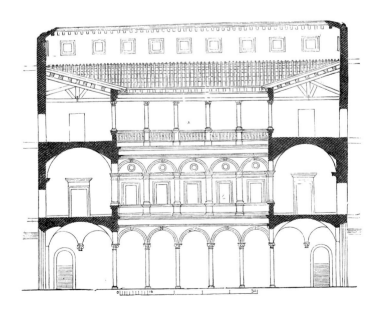

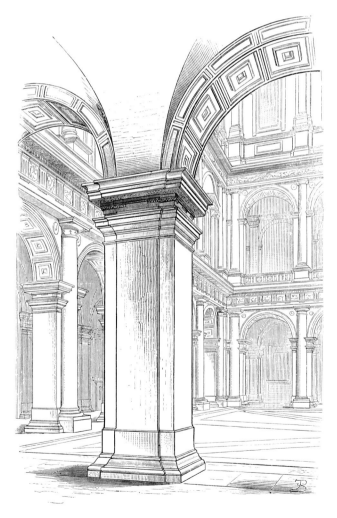

242

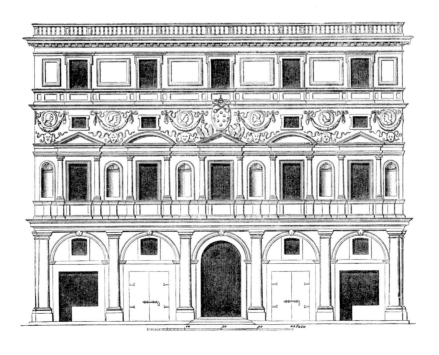

244

CAMERARIVS A SIXT III PONTIFICE MAXIMO HONORIBVS

0   5   10 M

247

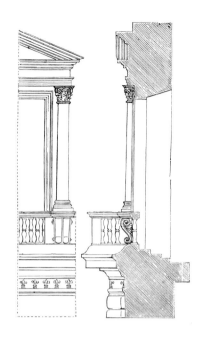

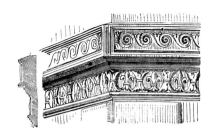

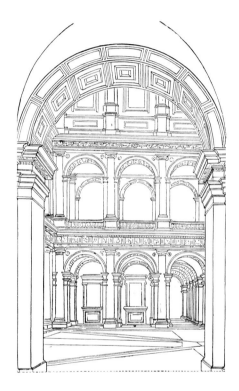

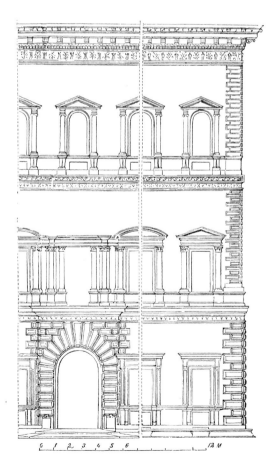

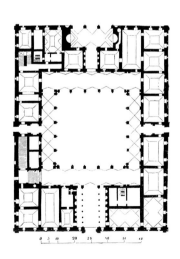

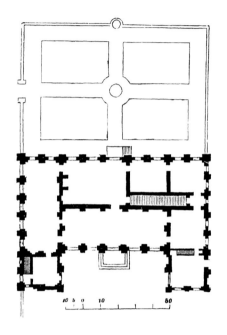

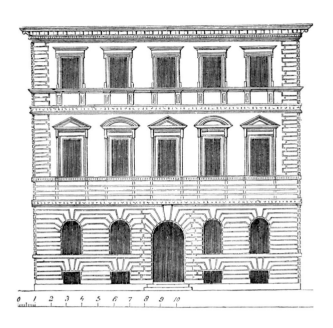

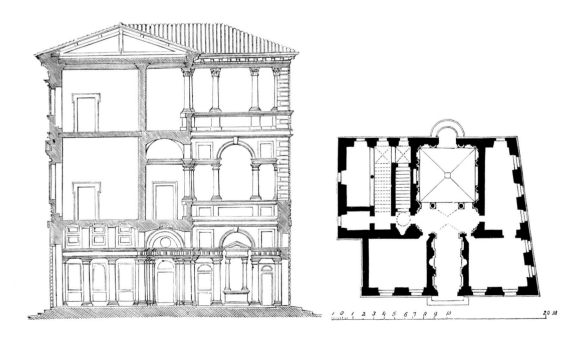

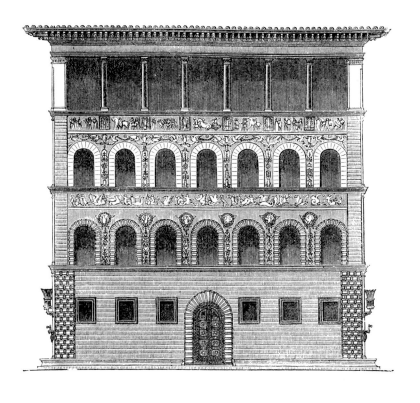

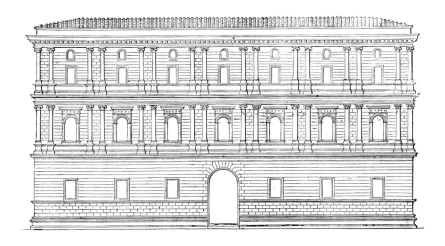

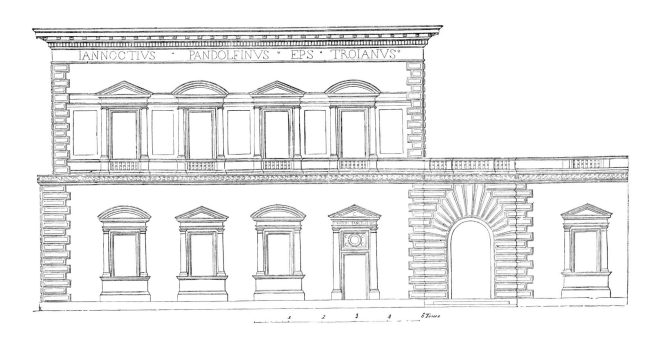

IANNOCTIVS · PANDOLFINVS · EPS · TROIANVS°

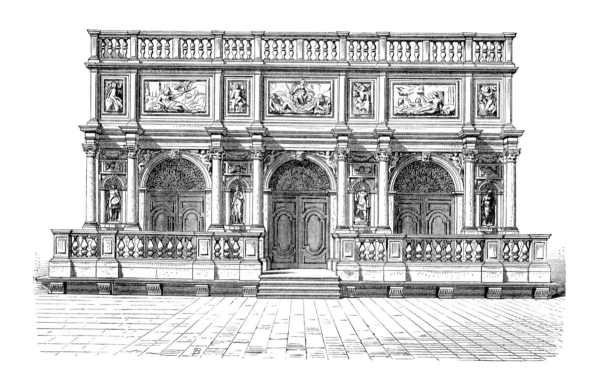

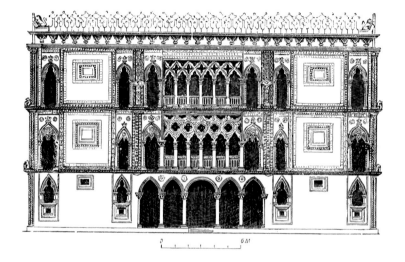

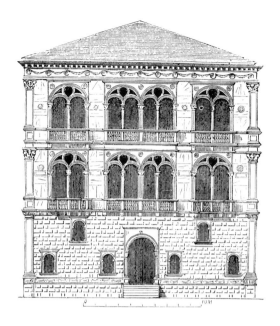

258

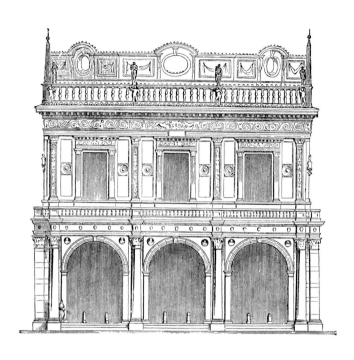

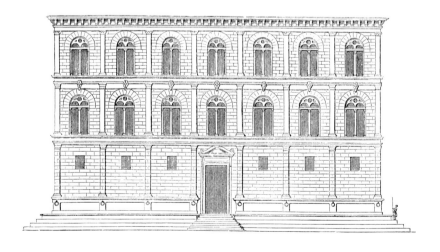

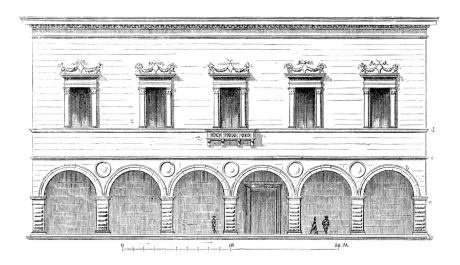

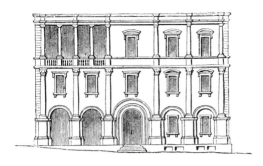

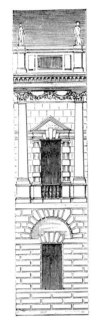

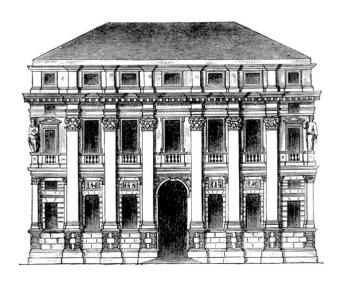

263

264

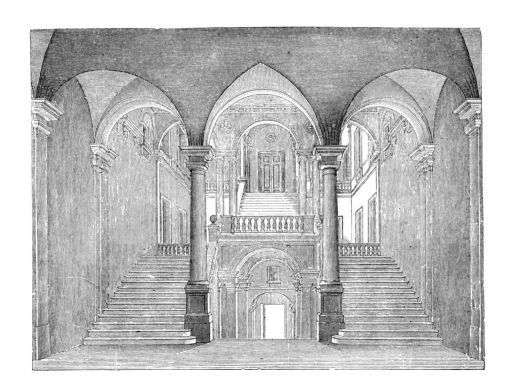

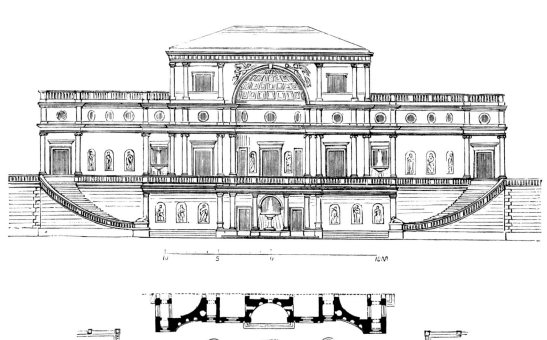

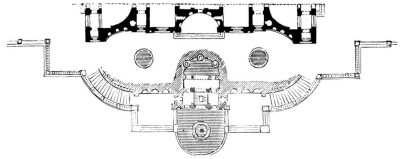

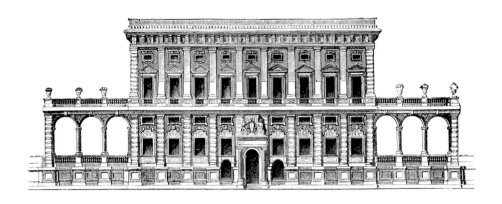

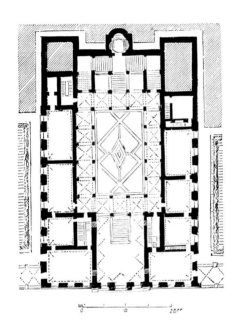

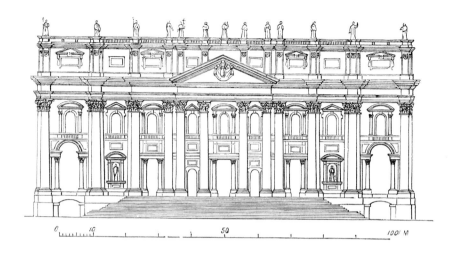

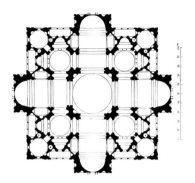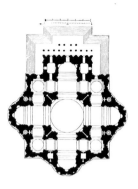

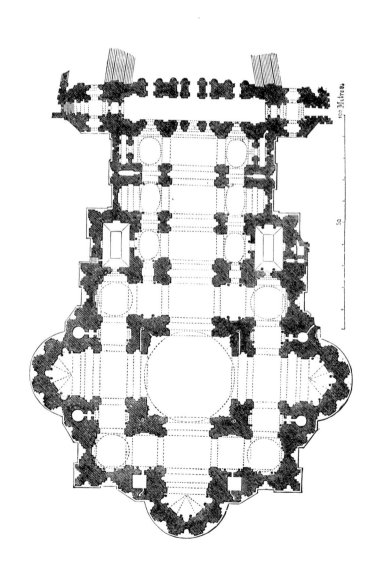

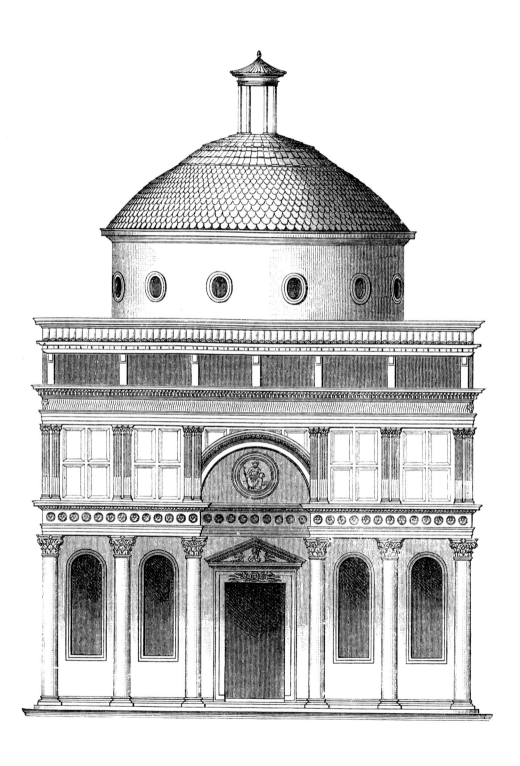

283

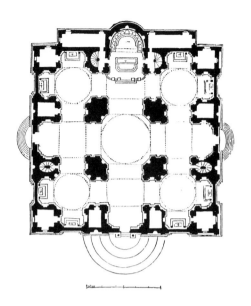

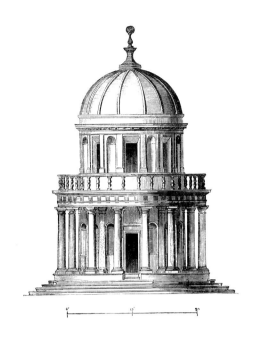

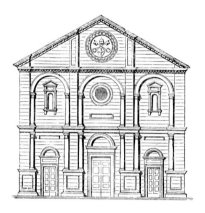

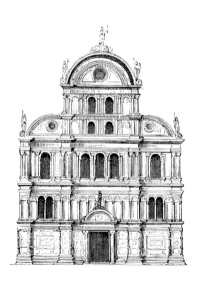

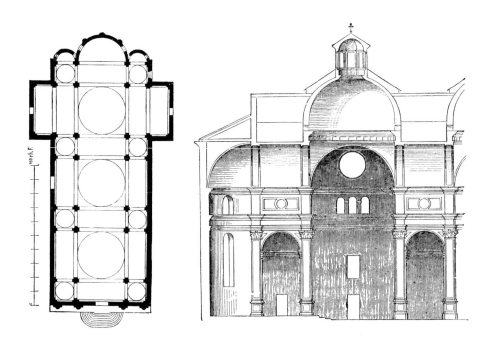

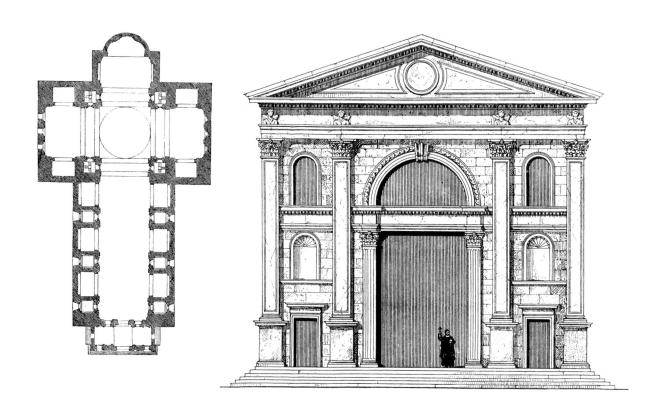

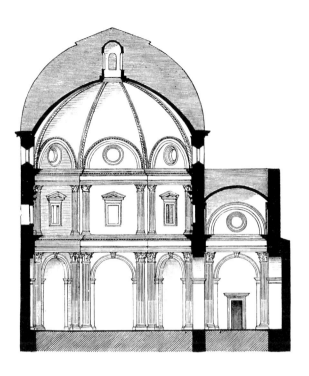

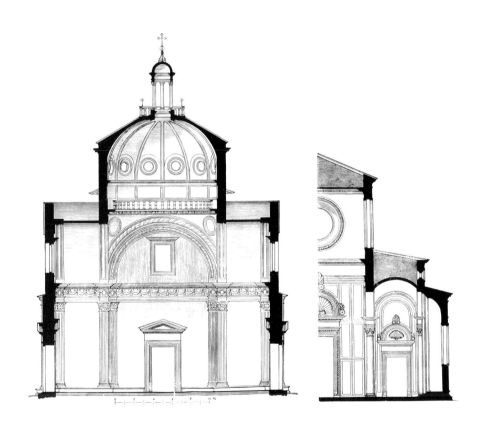

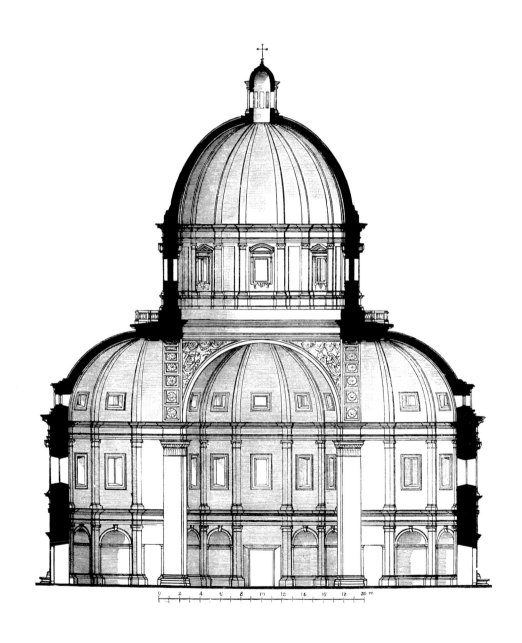

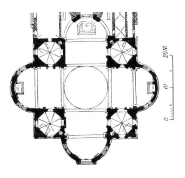

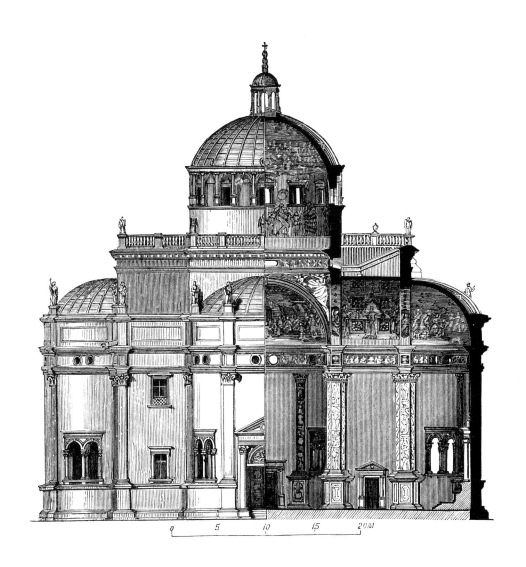

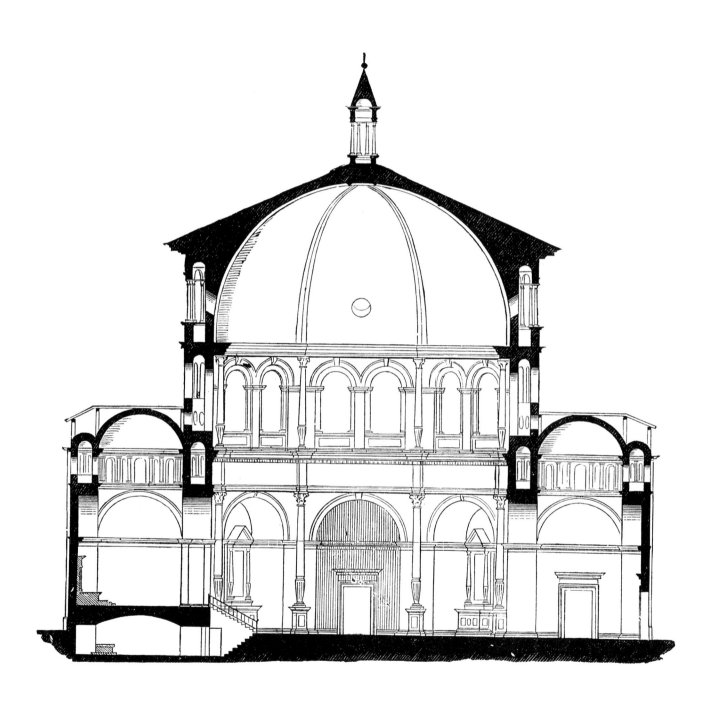

299

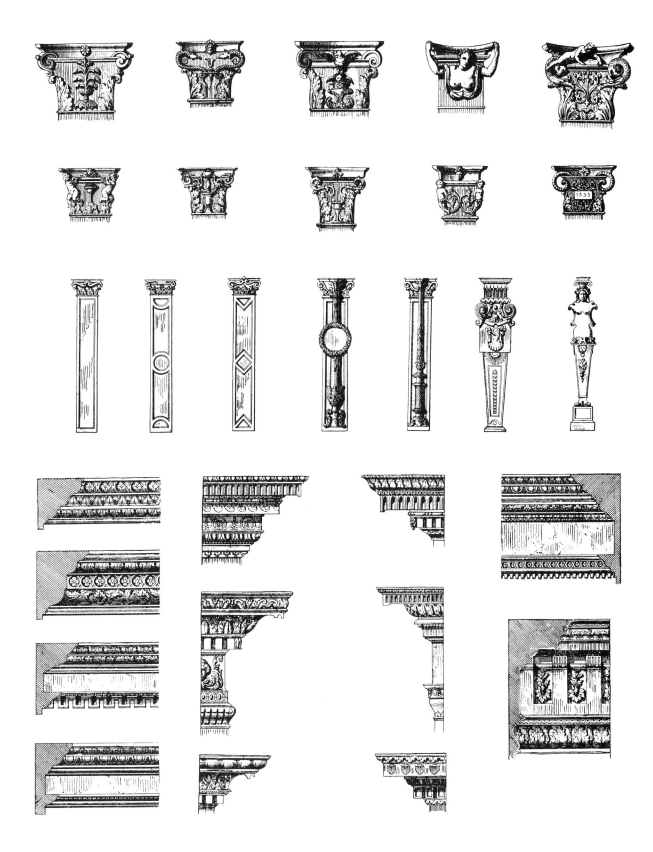

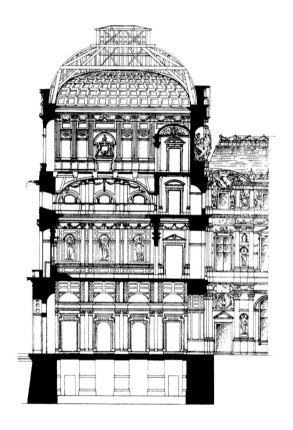

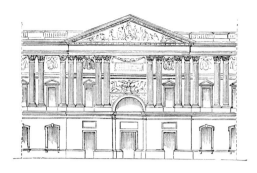

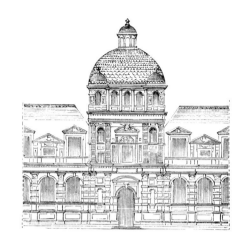

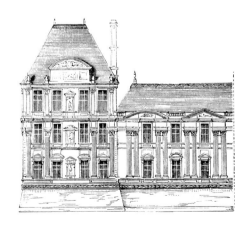

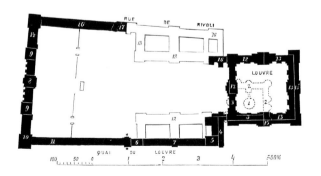

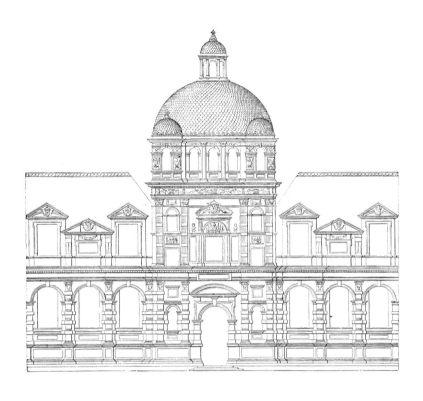

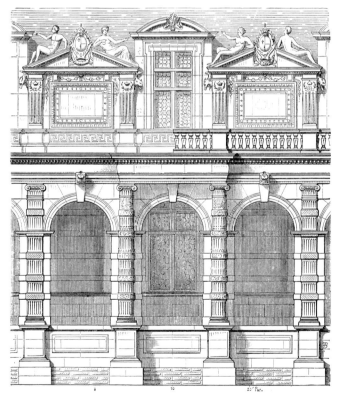

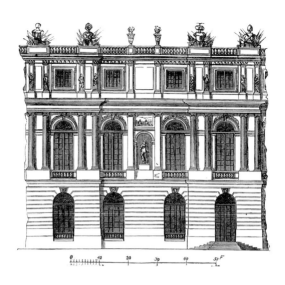

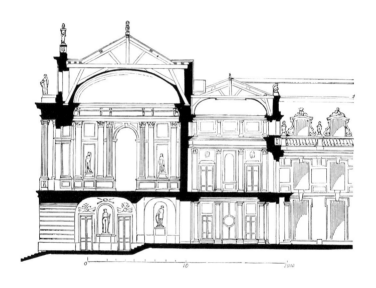

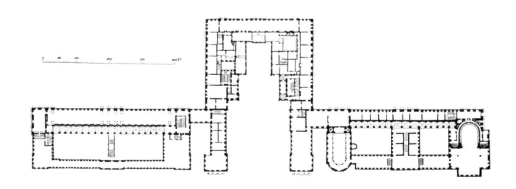

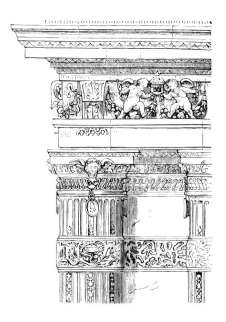

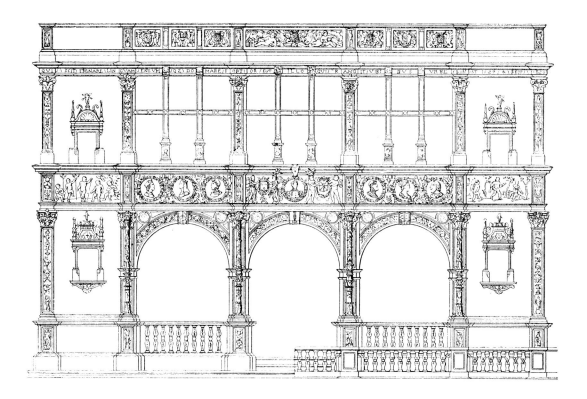

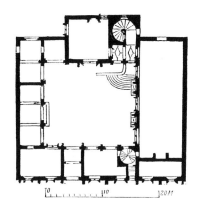

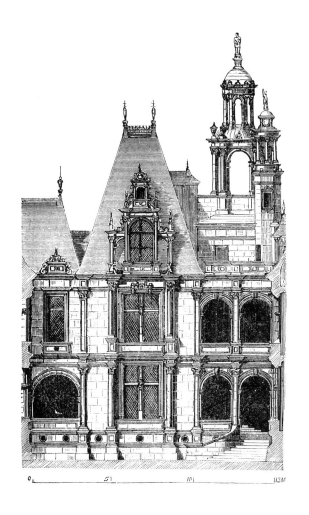

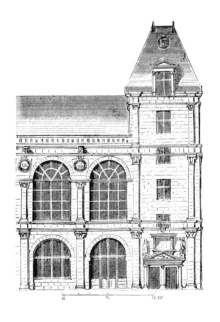

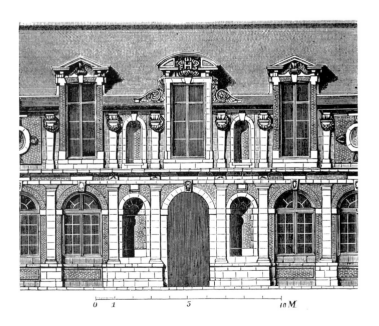

313

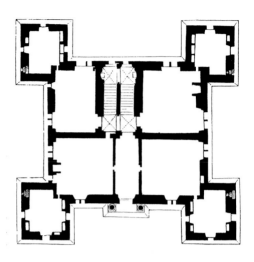

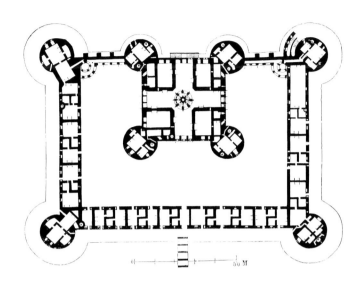

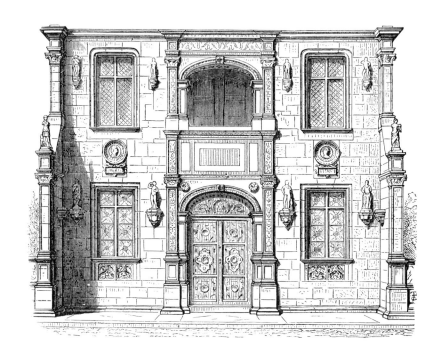

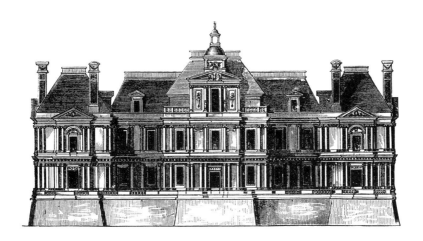

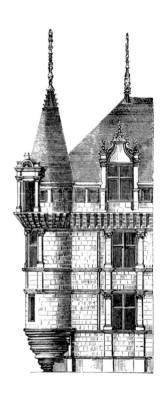

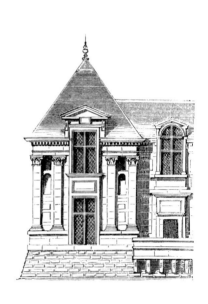

318

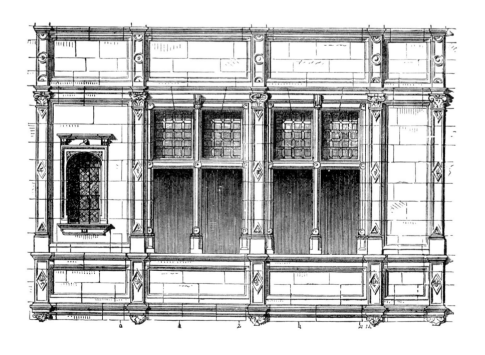

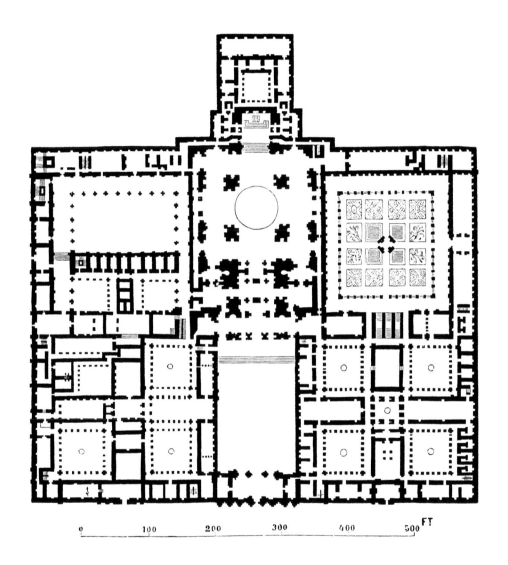

0   100   200   300   400   500 FT

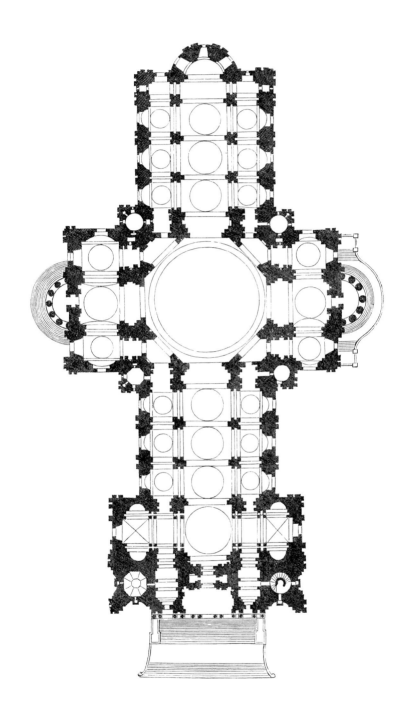

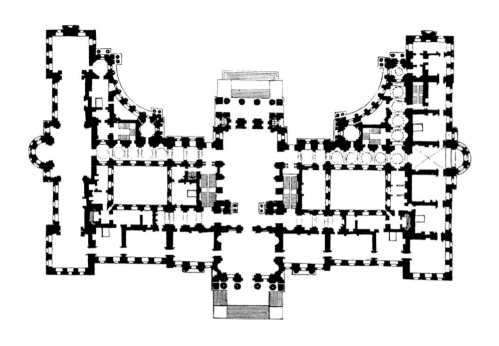

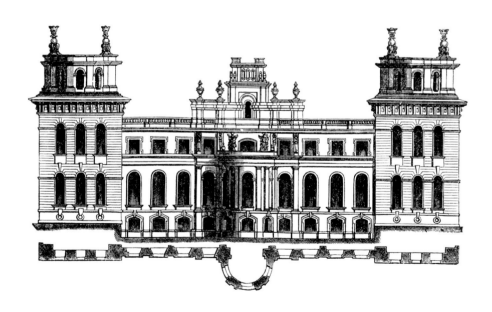

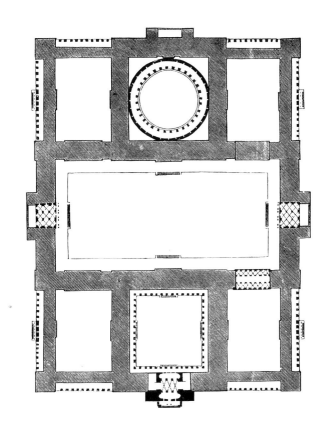

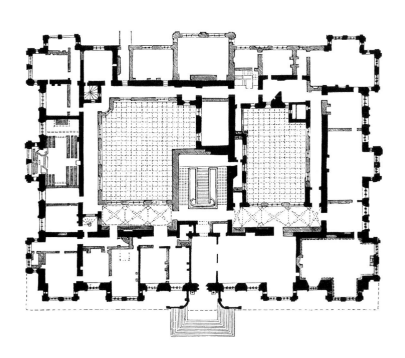

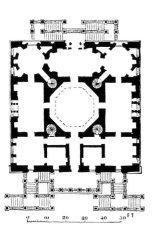

327

328

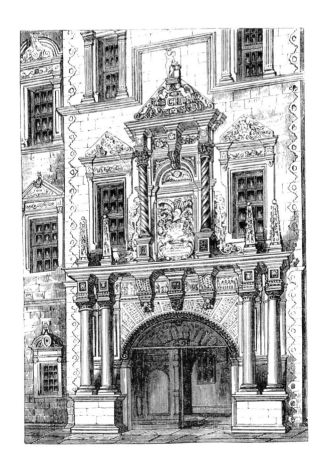

329

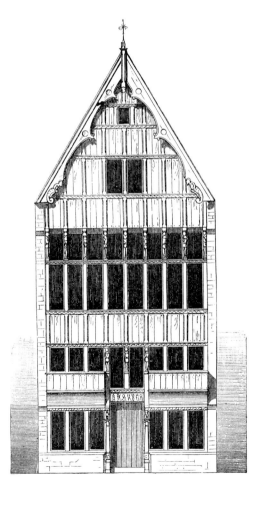

333

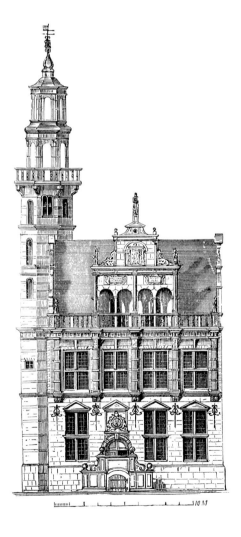

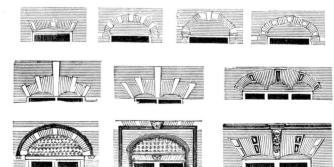

337

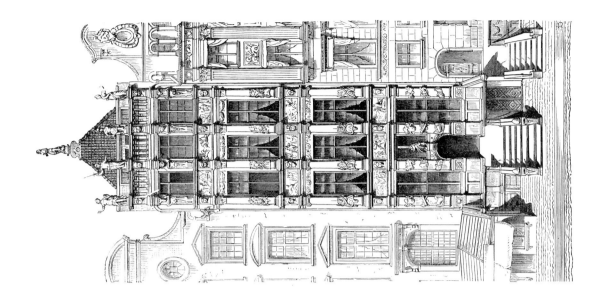

343

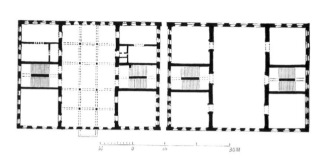

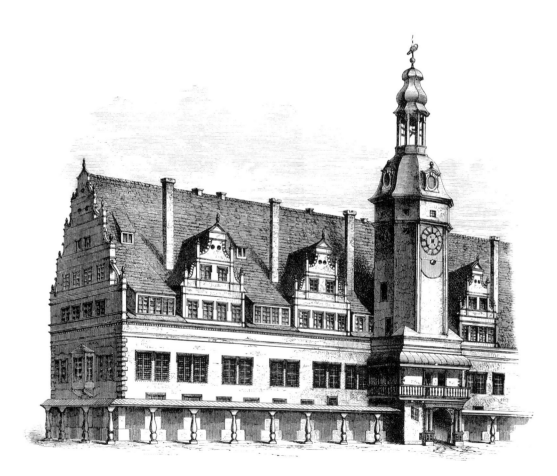

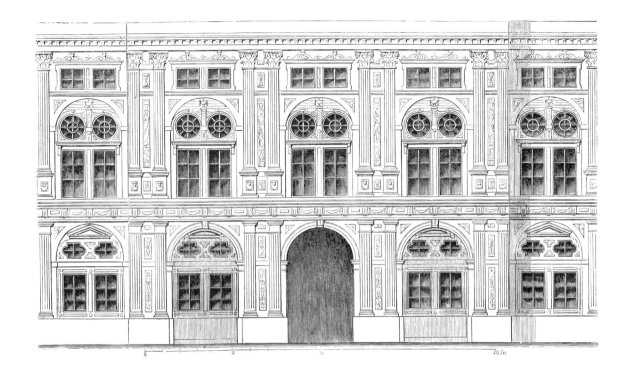

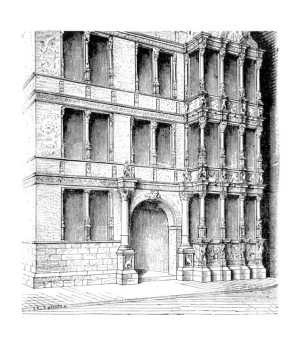

346

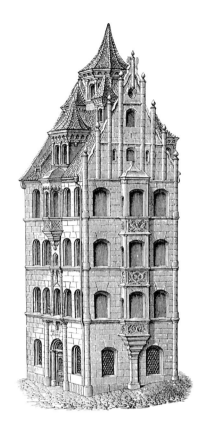

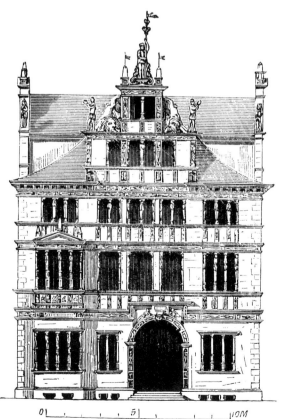

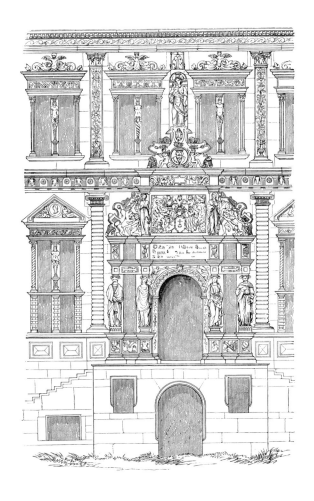

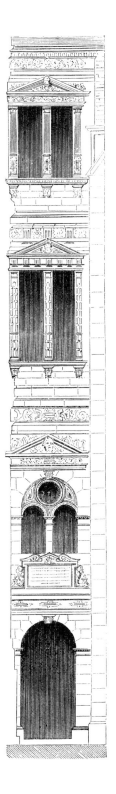

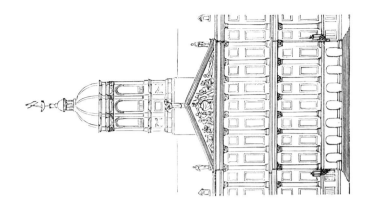

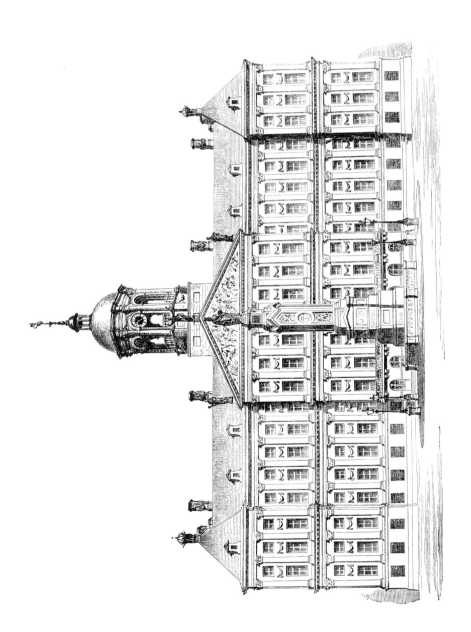

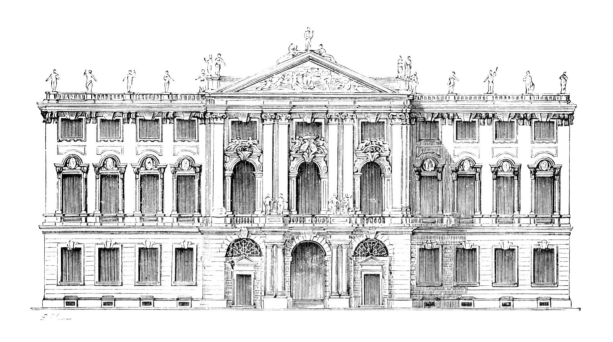

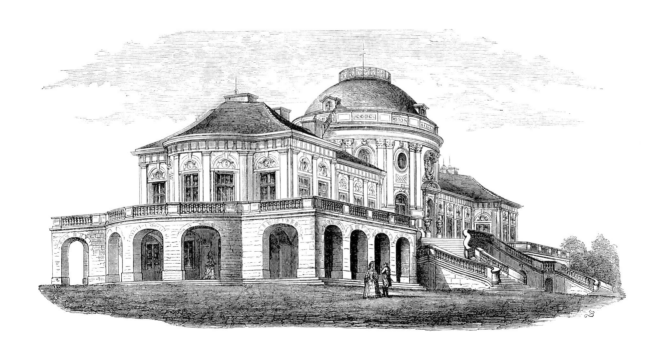

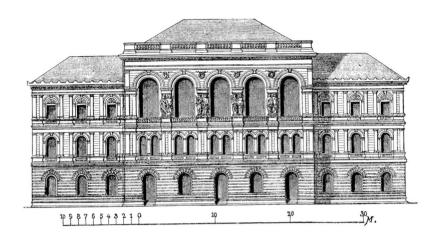

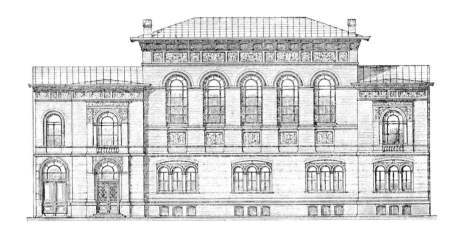

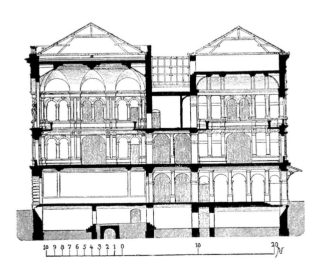

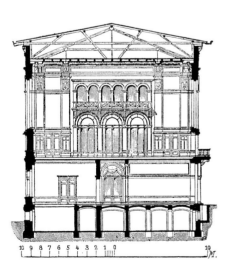

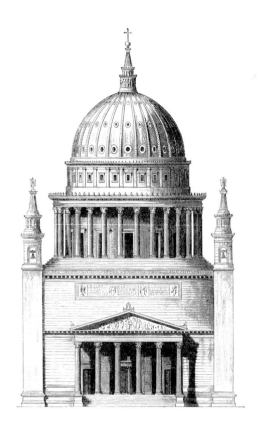

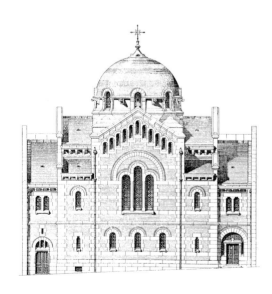

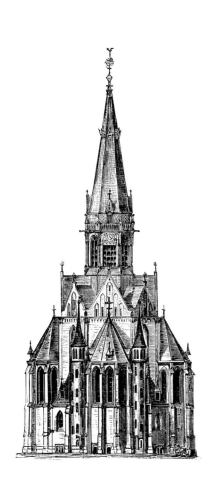

369

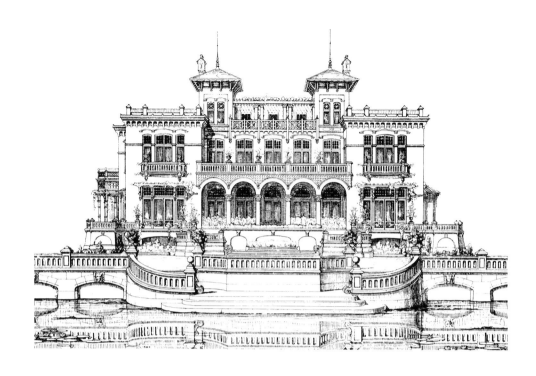

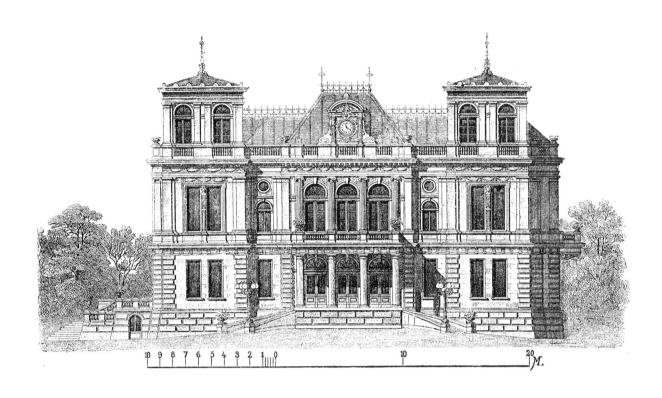

373

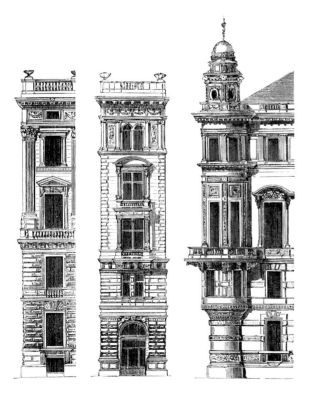
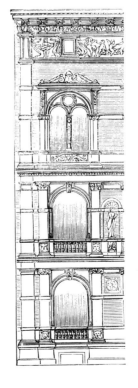

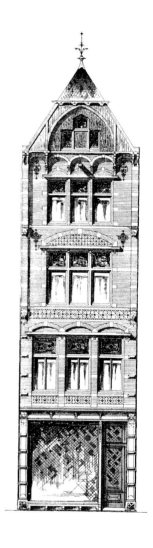

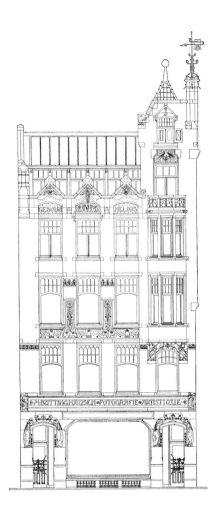

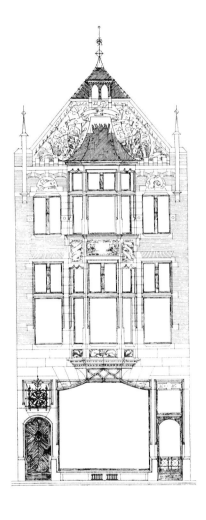

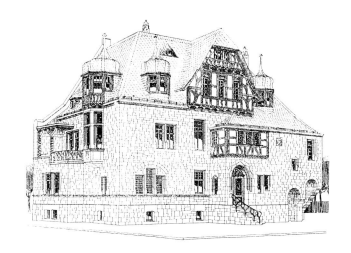

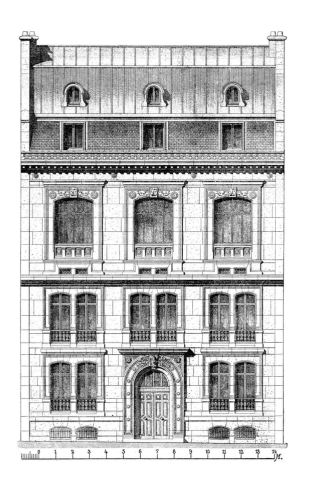

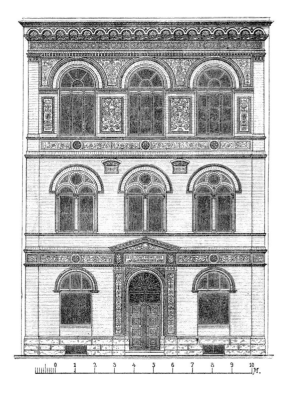

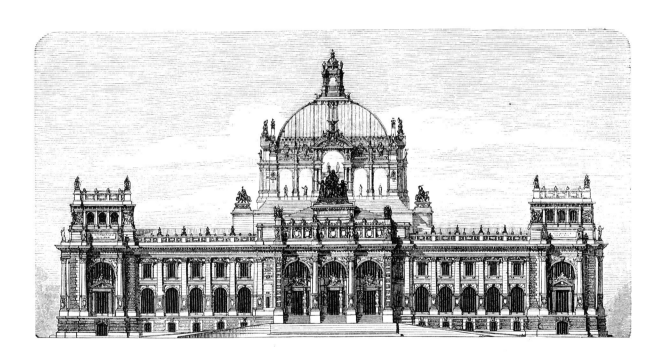

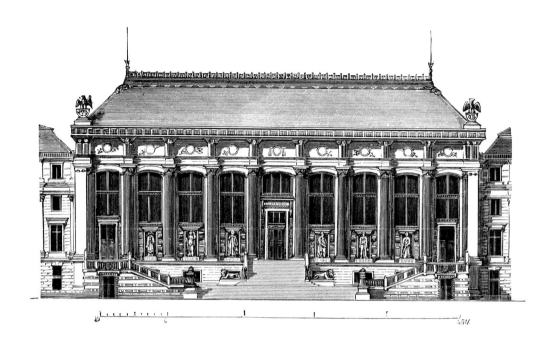

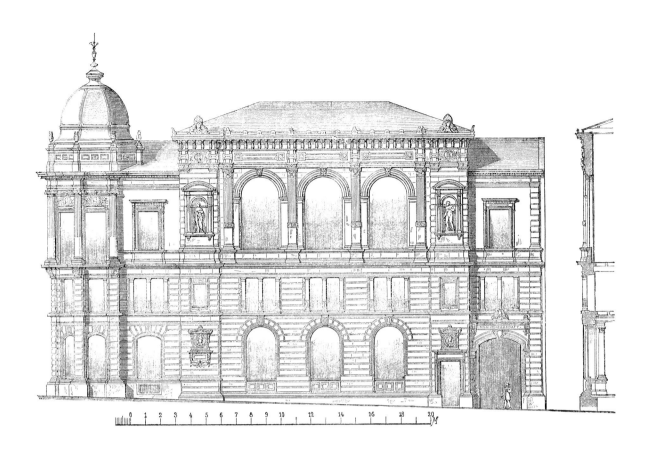

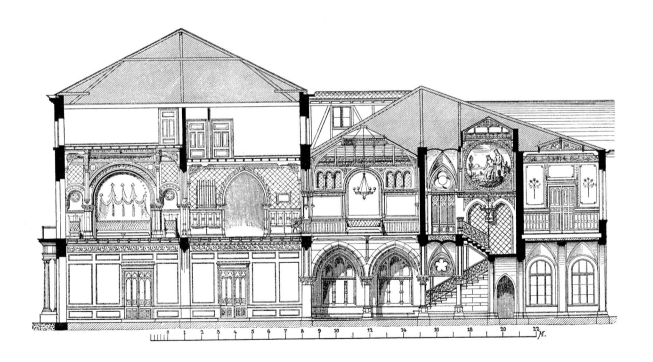

387

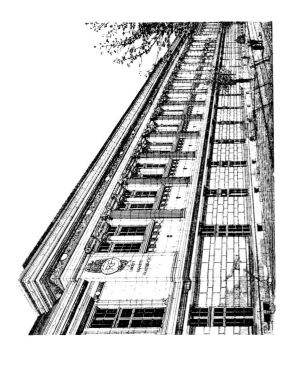

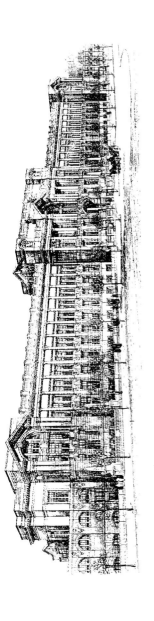

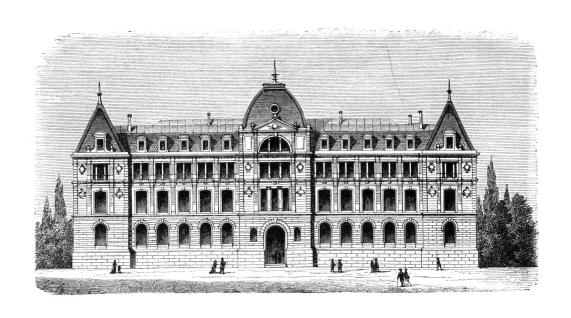

395

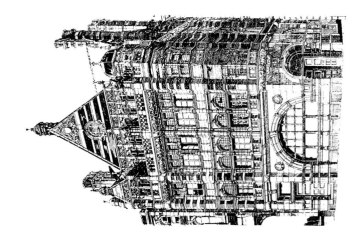

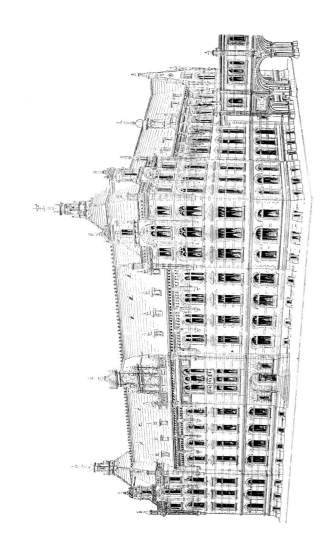

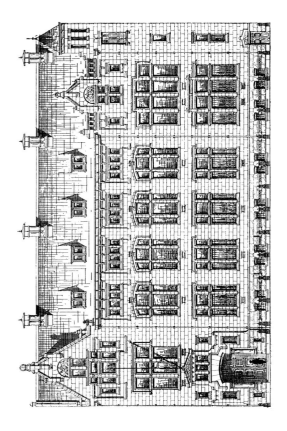

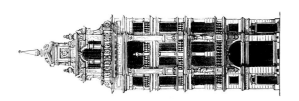

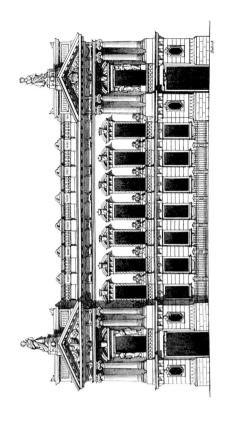

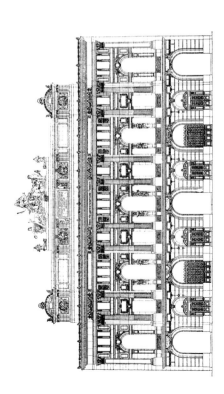

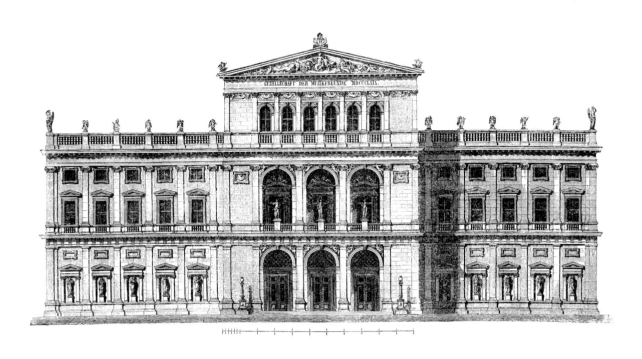

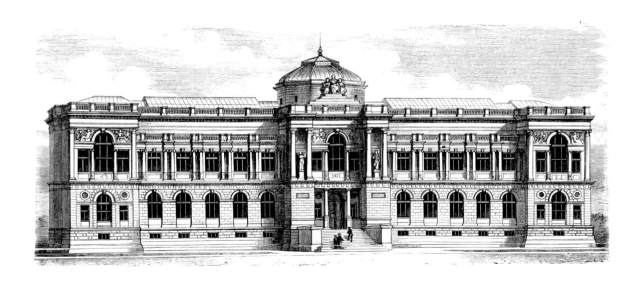

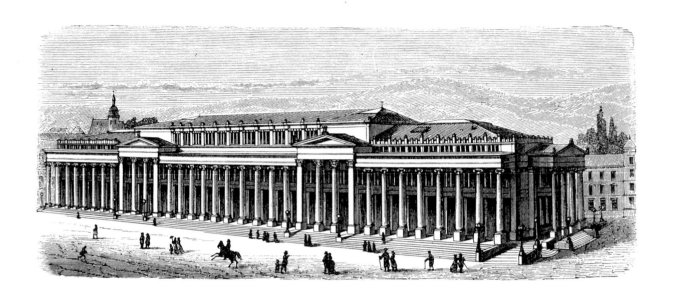

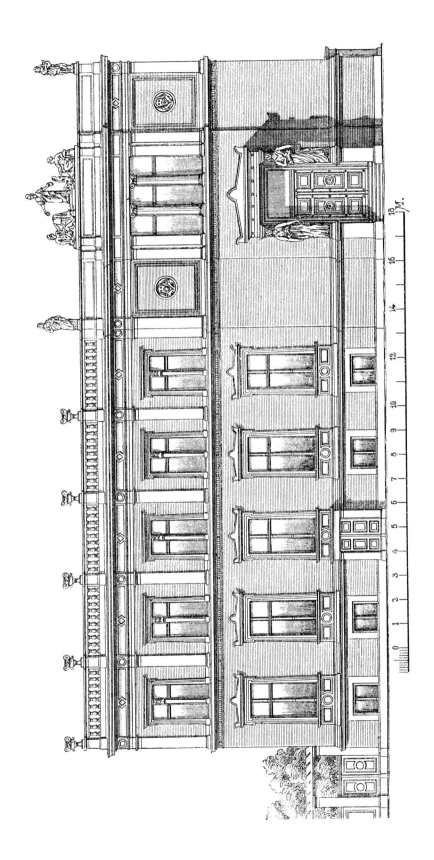

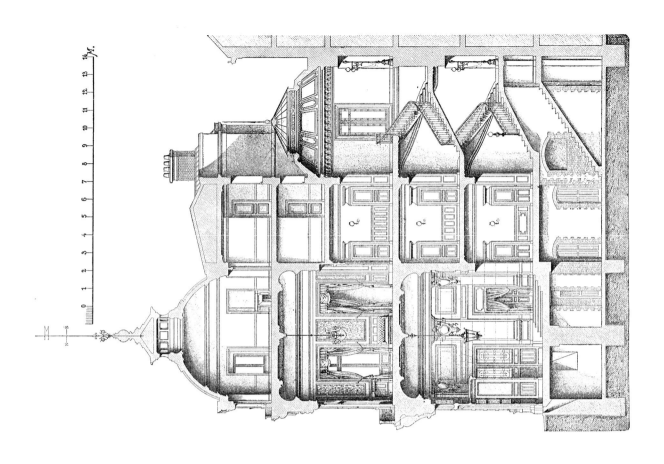

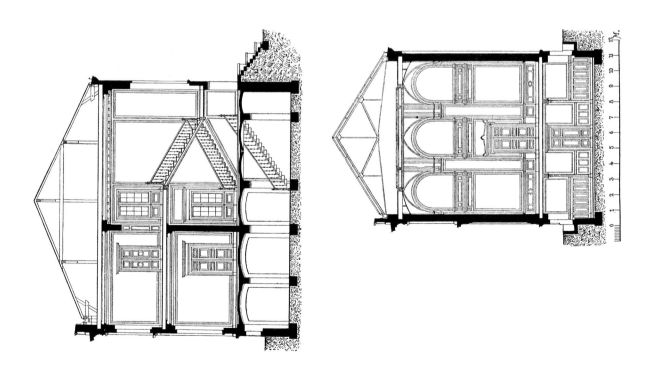

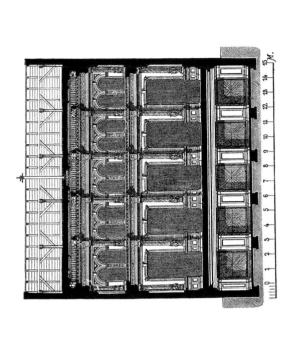

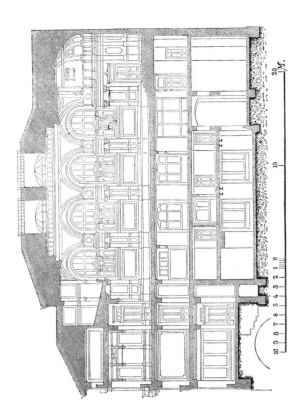

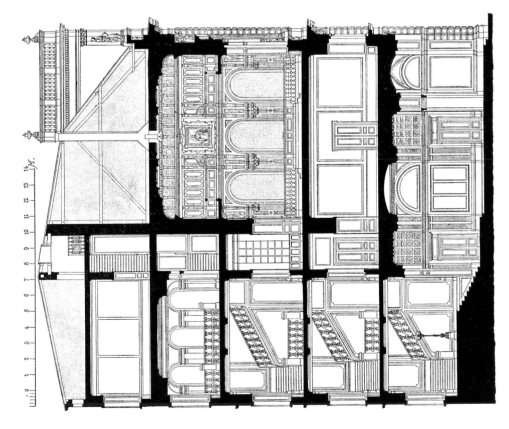

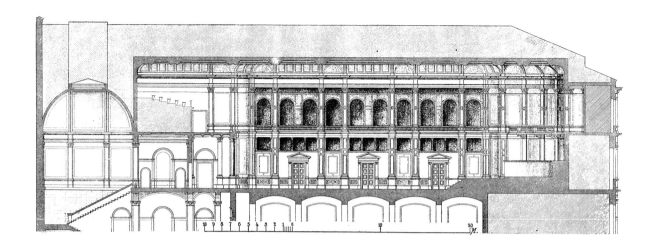

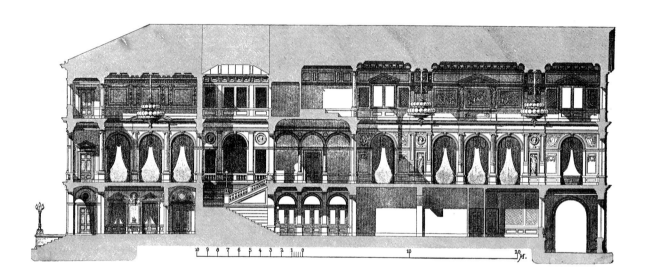

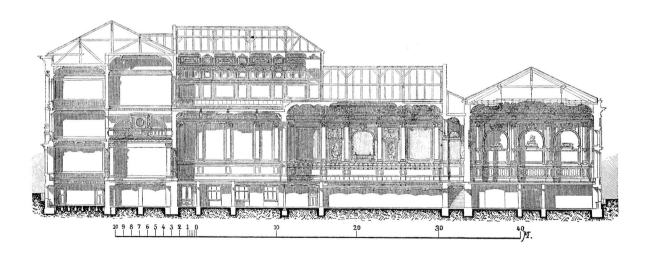

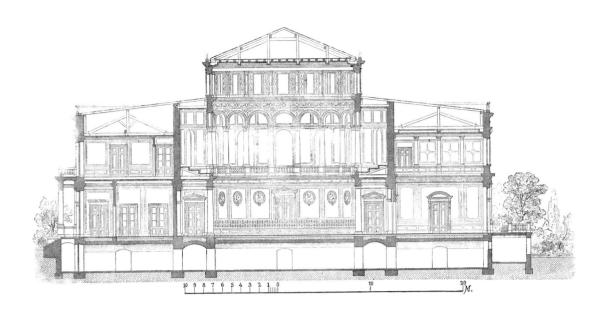

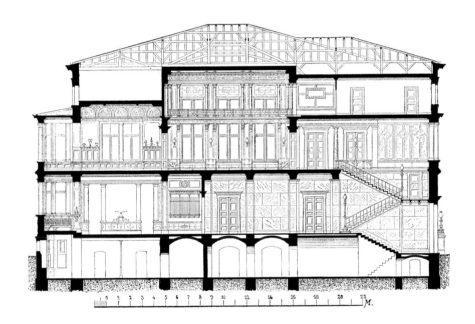

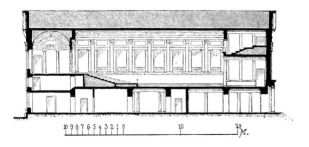

411

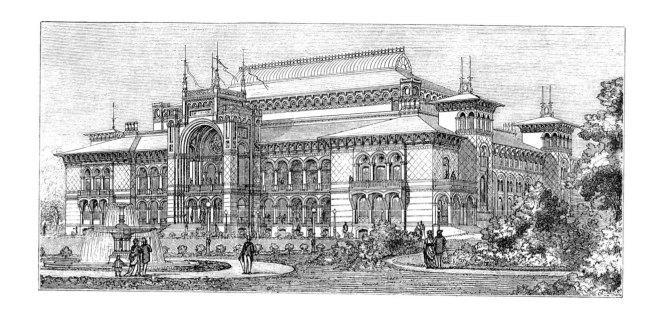

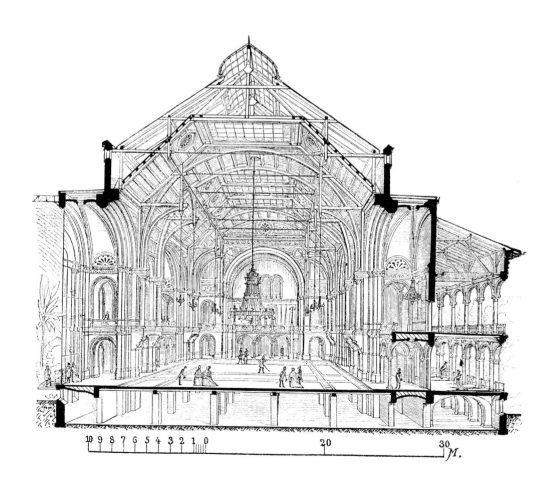

10 9 8 7 6 5 4 3 2 1 0   20   30 M.

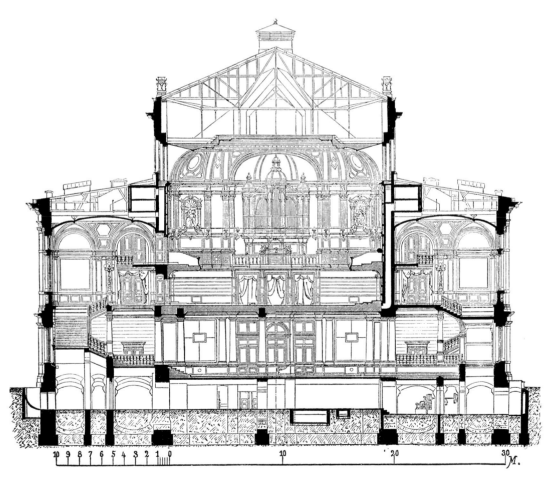

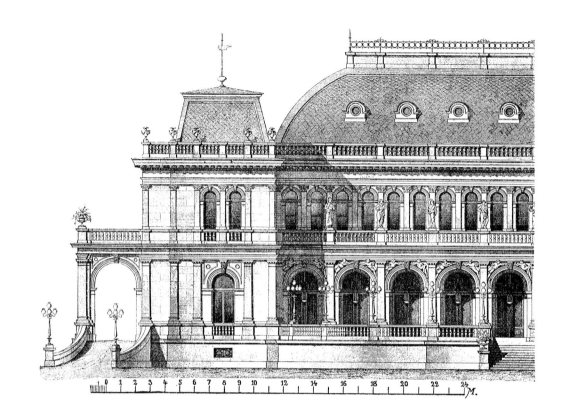

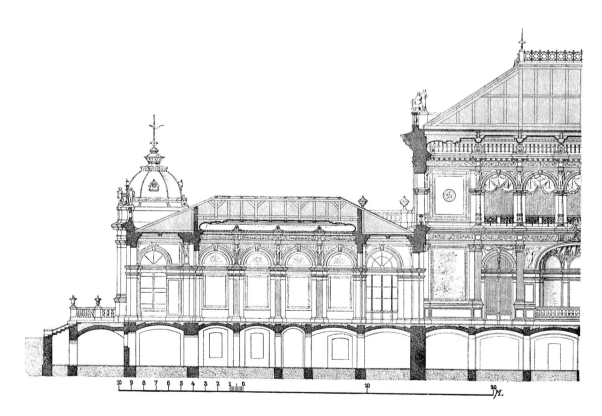

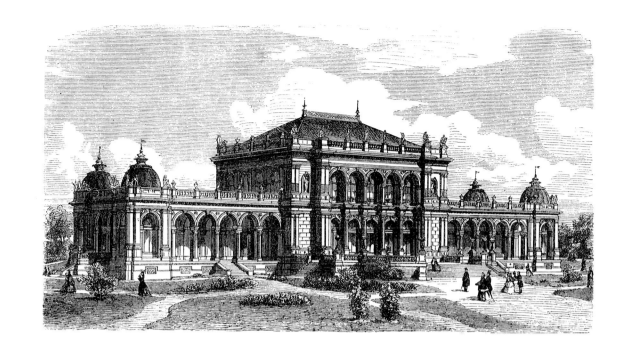

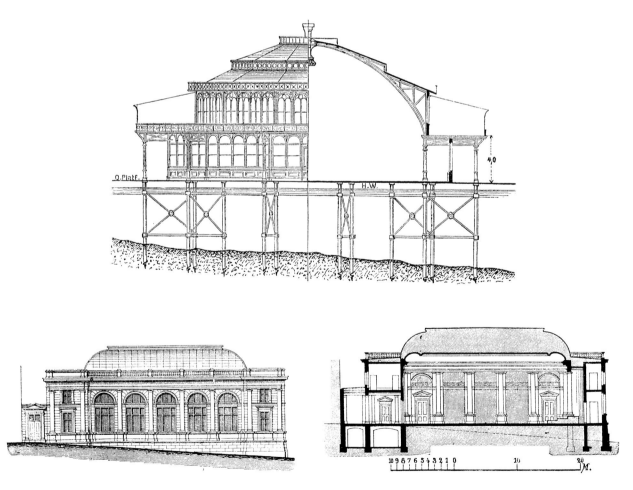

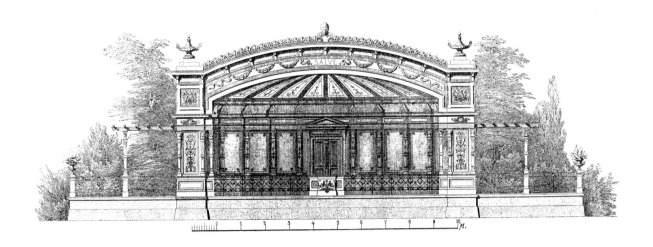

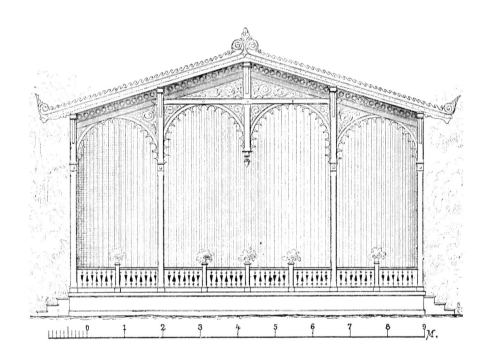

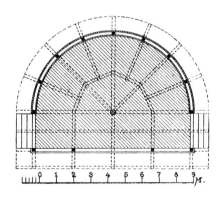

417

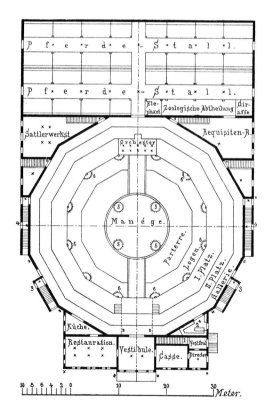

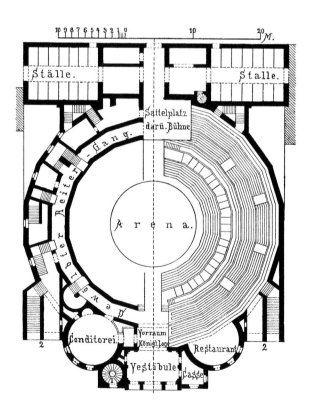

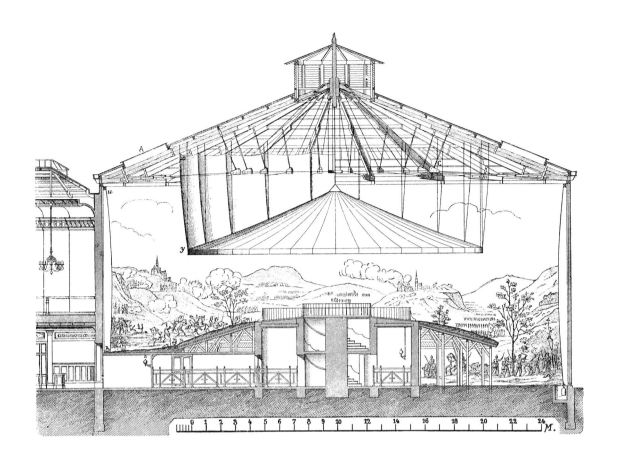

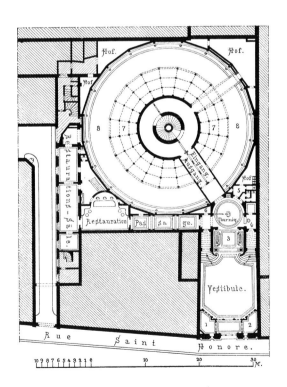

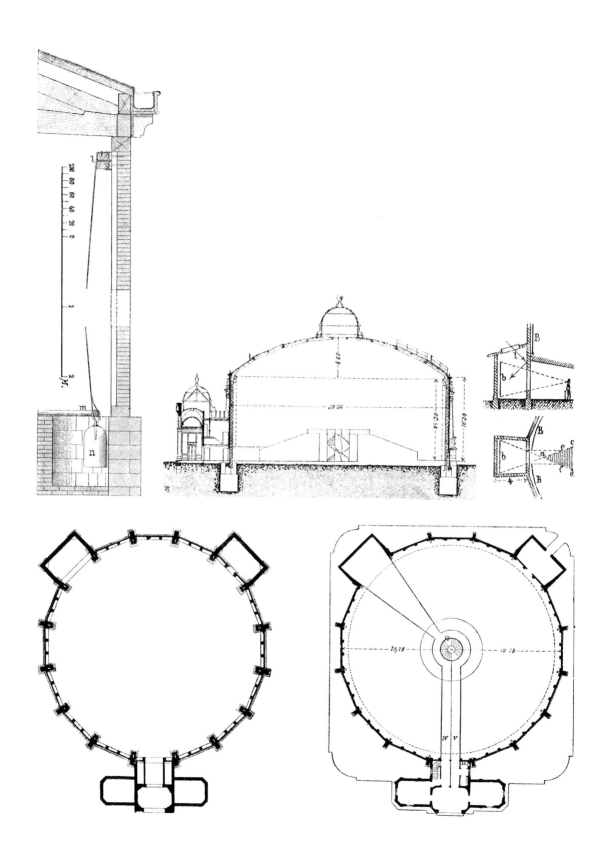

List of Buildings

PAGE 44: Ionic columns.

PAGE 45: Greek atlases from Agrigento, Italy (bottom left), and examples of Greek columns.

PAGE 46-47: Corinthian columns.

PAGE 48: Masonic roof construction of the Great Propylaea in Eleusis.

PAGE 49: Greek friezes.

PAGE 50: Greek doors and windows.

PAGE 51: Greek *acroterions*, roof ornaments.

PAGE 52: Mausoleum of Halicarnassus in Bodrum, Turkey.

PAGE 53: Lysicrates monument in Athens (left), and the rotunda of Arsinoë (right) at the island of Samothrace, Greece.

PAGE 54-55: Tomb in Tarquinia, Italy.

PAGE 56-57: Roman graves.

PAGE 58: Pyramid of Gaius Cestius in Rome (top left), Roman columns (top middle and right), well house in Tusculum (bottom left), and mouth of the Cloaca Maxima in Rome (bottom right).

PAGE 59: Gate in Volterra, Italy (top left), grave monument of St Remy in Arles, France (top right), grave of Caecilia Metella in Rome (center left), *hemicyclium* (center right), section and plan of a Roman *colombarium*, urn house (bottom).

PAGE 60-61: Roman bridges and aquaducts.

PAGE 62: Arches of Titus (top), and Constantine (bottom) in Rome.

PAGE 63: Temple of Hercules (top), and temple in Tivoli (bottom), Italy.

PAGE 64-65: Colosseum in Rome: view, four level floor plan, and longitudinal section.

PAGE 66: *Forum Romanum* in Rome.

PAGE 67: Pedestal, section and view of Trajan's Column in Rome.

PAGE 68-69: Plan, front view, and sections of the Pantheon in Rome.

PAGE 70-71: The Baths of Caracalla in Rome: plan (top left), central hall (bottom left), *tepidarium* (top right), cross section of the front building (center right), and longitudinal section of the main building (bottom right).

PAGE 72-73: Temple of Honos et Virtus in Rome: view (top left), longitudinal section (bottom left), cross section (top right), and plan (bottom right).

PAGE 74-75: Roman columns, capitals and friezes.

PAGE 76-77: *Teatro comico* in Pompeii, Italy (top left), Roman theatre (bottom left) of Aspendos (Belkis, Turkey), section of the Roman theatre in Orange, France (top right), Roman theatre in Segesta, Italy (bottom right).

PAGE 78-79: Sections and plans of three private houses in Pompeii, Italy.

PAGE 80: Interior of the small theatre of Pompeii, Italy.

PAGE 81: Interior of a Roman private house.

PAGE 82: Palace of emperor Diocletian in Spalato (Split, Croatia): partial view, detail of the façade, and plan.

PAGE 83: Porta Nigra (Black Gate) in Trier, Germany (top), and grave monument of Caecilia Metella at the Via Appia in Rome (bottom).

PAGE 84: Papal crypt.

PAGE 85: Entrance of the catacombs of S. Callisto (top), and an *arcosolium,* a niche with a martyr's grave (bottom).

PAGE 86: Cosmate columns from the monastery of S. Paolo near Rome (left), and view of the choir of Monreale Cathedral (right).

PAGE 205: Plan and view of Milan Cathedral, Italy.

PAGE 206-207: From left to right: Elevations of the naves of S. Mary in Beverley, and of Beverly Minster, Great Britain, elevations of the exteriors of Utrecht Cathedral, The Netherlands, and Cologne Cathedral, Germany; elevations of the naves of Soissons Cathedral, France, Utrecht Cathedral, The Netherlands and Cologne Cathedral, Germany.

PAGE 208: Cross section of choir of a church in Zwettl, Austria (top left), cross section of Ste Chapelle in Paris (top right), cross sections of two Gothic churches (bottom).

PAGE 209: Gothic abbey (top left), Beauvais Cathedral, France (top right), 's-Hertogenbosch Cathedral, The Netherlands (bottom left), and Soissons Cathedral, France (bottom right).

PAGE 210-211: Gothic spires.

PAGE 212: Portals from St Martin in Colmar, France (top), and St Sebald in Nuremberg, Germany (bottom).

PAGE 213: Gallery of Amiens Cathedral, France (top), and portal of the Romanesque church in Thann, France (bottom).

PAGE 214: Interiors of Ste Madeleine in Troyes, France (top left), Alby Cathedral, France (top right), Strassburg Cathedral, France (bottom left and right).

PAGE 215-223: Details of Gothic cathedrals: arches and vaults, columns, capitals, bases, and windows.

PAGE 224: Houses in Amiens, France (left) and Rouen, France (right).

PAGE 225: France (from left to right, top to bottom): Presbytery in Vendôme, house of Jacques Coeur in Bourges, donjon of Poitiers, and house in Sens.

PAGE 226: *Schauhaus* in Nuremberg, Germany (top) and Town Hall of Braunschweig, Germany (bottom).

PAGE 227: Germany: Monastery in Einsiedln (top), Holsten Tower in Lübeck (bottom left), Eschenheimer Tower in Frankfurt a.M. (bottom center), and tower in Wismar (bottom right).

PAGE 228: Spahlen Tower in Basel, Switzerland (top), and Nassau House in Nuremberg, Germany (bottom).

PAGE 229: House in Greifswald, Germany (top), and *Das steinerne Haus* in Frankfurt a.M., Germany (bottom).

PAGE 230: Town Hall of Louvain, Belgium.

PAGE 231: Town Hall of Lübeck, Germany (top left), Town Hall of Wernigerode (bottom left), and Town Hall of Münster, Germany (right).

PAGE 232: Cloth Hall in Ypres, Belgium (top), and houses in Delft, The Netherlands, in Bruges, Belgium and in Mechelen, Belgium (bottom left, center and middle).

PAGE 233: Warwick Castle, Great Britain (top left), Marburg Castle, Germany (top right), and Casa Lonja in Valencia, Spain (bottom).

PAGE 234: Italy: Cà d'Oro in Venice (top), and a house in S. Gimignano (bottom).

PAGE 235: Italy: Elevation of the nave of S. Petronio in Bologna (top left), interior and exterior of Lucca Cathedral (top center and right), *Palazzo pubblico* in Udine (center), courtyard of a small house in Genoa (bottom left), and Broletto in Monza (bottom right).

PAGE 236: Italy: City gate of S. Gimignano (top), Bigallo in Florence (bottom left), and exterior of the Palazzo Buonsignori in Siena (bottom right).

PAGE 237: Plan, exterior and courtyard façade of the Palazzo Visconti in Pavia, Italy.

PAGE 345: *Kaiserhof* in the *Residenz* in Munich, Germany (top), and Town Hall of Mühlhausen, France (bottom).

PAGE 346: Guild-hall in Basel, Switzerland (top left), *Stadtweinhaus* in Münster, Germany (top right), *Von Leibnitz Haus* in Hannover, Germany, *Altes Rathaus* (Old Town Hall) in Cologne, Germany (bottom right).

PAGE 347: *Seidenhof* in Zürich, Switzerland (top left), *Peller's Haus* in Nuremberg, Germany (top right), *Das Zeughaus* in Gdańsk, Poland (bottom left), and private house in Nuremberg, Germany (bottom right).

PAGE 348: *Topler'sches Haus* in Nuremberg, Germany (top left), Wedekind House in Hildesheim, Germany (top right), House of the Fathers in Hannover, Germany (bottom left), and *Peller Haus* in Nuremberg (bottom right).

PAGE 349: Heidelberg Castle, Germany.

PAGE 350: Room in Trausnitz Castle near Landshut, Germany.

PAGE 351: 16th century interior of a German house.

PAGE 352: 16th century interior of a Belgian house.

PAGE 353: Royal Palace (former Town Hall) in Amsterdam.

PAGE 354: Courtyard of the *Berliner Schloss* (top), and courtyard of the *koniglicher Schloss* in Berlin (bottom).

PAGE 355: Decorated window in the *Berliner Schloss*.

PAGE 356: Façade of the *Berliner Zeughaus*, the former arsenal.

PAGE 357: Trautson Palace (top), and a villa near Stuttgart, Germany (bottom).

PAGE 358: *Französischer Dom* in Berlin (top), and St Gallen Cathedral (bottom).

PAGE 359: *Vierzehnheiligen*, pilgrimage church in Franconia.

PAGE 360: Pavilion of the *Residenz* in Würzburg, Germany.

PAGE 361: Western pavilion of the *Zwinger* in Dresden, Germany.

PAGE 362: Interior of the *Amalienburg* in the Nymphenburger Park, Munich, Germany.

PAGE 363: Casino building (top), clubhouse in Wroclaw, Poland (center), and their cross sections (bottom).

PAGE 364: St Nicholas in Potsdam, Germany (top left), St Michael in Berlin (top right), St Thomas in Berlin (bottom left), and Greek Church in Paris (bottom right).

PAGE 365: Union Church in Brighton, Great Britain (top left), St Augustin in Paris (top right), Ste Madeleine in Paris (bottom left), and city church (bottom right).

PAGE 366: *Votivkirche* in Vienna.

PAGE 367: Church in Fünfhaus near Vienna.

PAGE 368: *Mariahilfkirche* near Münich, Germany (left), and St Peter in Berlin (right).

PAGE 369: *Kerk van het Heilige Hart* (Holy Hart Church) in Amsterdam (left), and Reformed Church in Katwijk aan Zee, The Netherlands (right).

PAGE 370: Castle Oud-Wassenaar in The Netherlands (top), and Villa Siegle near Stuttgart, Germany (bottom).

PAGE 371: Schwerin Castle, Germany.

PAGE 372: Villa Ma Retraite in Zeist, The Netherlands (top), and Palais Helfert in Vienna (bottom).

PAGE 373: Casino in Karlstadt, Germany (top), House of the Carlton Club in London (center), and clubhouse in Berlin (bottom).

PAGE 374: Corner building in Paris (top left), corner building in Budapest (top right), Château Bérenger in Paris (bottom left), and a private house in Antwerp (bottom right).

PAGE 375: *Königliches Hofbräuhaus* in Munich, Gemany (top), elevations of three houses in Vienna (bottom left) and three houses in Berlin (bottom right).

PAGE 376-377: 19th century Dutch shops.

PAGE 378: 19th century villas.

PAGE 379: 19th century villas in Paris (top left), Karlsruhe, Germany (top right), in Huddersfield, Great Britain (bottom left), and Paris (bottom right).

PAGE 380: Clubhouse of the Society of Civil Engineers in Paris (left), and clubhouse in Kiel, Germany (right).

Page 381: Clubhouse of the Geographic Society in Paris (left), and *Adeliges Casino* in Vienna (right).

PAGE 382: Houses of Parliament in London.

PAGE 383: *Reichstag* (parliament building) in Vienna (top), and Berlin (bottom).

PAGE 384: Law courts in Paris: façade with main entrance (top), and *Salle des pas perdus* (bottom).

PAGE 385: Law courts in Brussels.

PAGE 386: Law courts in Munich, Germany (top), and in London (bottom).

PAGE 387: Clubhouses in Stuttgart, Germany (top), and Aachen, Germany (bottom).

PAGE 388: Reading-room of the National Library in Paris.

PAGE 389: Staircase of the National Library in Munich, Germany.

PAGE 390: Anatomy Building in Berlin (top left), Medicine Faculty in Paris (top right), Royal College of Science in South Kensington, Great Britain (bottom).

PAGE 391: Academy of Science in Athens.

PAGE 392: Polytechnic College in Munich, Germany: façade (top), and staircase (bottom).

PAGE 393: Grammar school in Hildesheim, Germany (top), *Baugewerkenschule* in Stuttgart, Germany (bottom).

PAGE 394: The *Rijksmuseum* in Amsterdam (top), and *Altes Museum* in Berlin (bottom).

PAGE 395: Elevation and view of the *Hofmuseum* in Vienna.

PAGE 396: *Petit palais des Beaux-Arts* in Paris (top), and arcades in the *österreichischen Museums für Kunst und Industrie* in Vienna (bottom).

PAGE 397: Former Jewish Hospital in Amsterdam (top), and entrance hall of the railway station in Stuttgart, Germany (bottom).

PAGE 398: Bank in Amsterdam (top left), City Bank, Ludgate Hill, London (top right), Belgian Bank in Brussels (bottom left), and building of the National Dutch Railway Company in Utrecht, The Netherlands (bottom right).

Page 399: Exchange in Berlin (top right), and Brussels (bottom left), National Bank in Brussels (bottom left), *Börse für landwirtschaftliche Producte* in Vienna (bottom right).

PAGE 400: *Meininger Bank* in Berlin.

PAGE 401: Concerthall in Vienna (top), and *Städelsches Institut & Stadtische Galerie* in Frankfurt a.M., Germany.

PAGE 402: *Königsbau* in Stuttgart, Germany (top), and *Frankfurter Hof* in Frankfurt a.M., Germany (bottom).

PAGE 403: 19th century clubhouse in Kassel, Germany.

PAGE 404-407: Sections of 19th century clubhouses, concert halls, a Freemason's lodge, a music acadamy, and a casino.

PAGE 408: *Comptoir National d'escompte* in Paris.

PAGE 409: *Befreiungshalle* in Kehlheim.